More Praise for *How Performance Management Is Killing Performance—and What to Do About It*

"I place inordinate value in business books that are first and foremost practical. Tamra met my high bar and then some. I'm a CEO, not an HR leader, and I can't wait to share this framework with my leadership team. It is a great way to talk about helping our people thrive and grow themselves in a terrific combination of head and heart. Dig in! You'll be glad you did."
—Steve Trautman, CEO, The Steve Trautman Company

"Performance management has been like the frog slowly dying as the water temperature rises. Lately the pot is boiling over and companies sense that traditional performance management is dead. But many lack the confidence and know-how to replace it with a vibrant and sophisticated system that endures. Enter Tamra, who offers a vibrant framework to balance three demands: organizationally aligned goals, development, and rewards. She gives an elegant starting point for a strategically customized solution that fits with business strategy and culture. And she goes much further, laying out models, templates, and a step-by-step map to move from high-level design to tactical implementation. If you are going to change performance management, get this indispensable guide to do it right."
—Jeannie Coyle, coauthor of *Make Talent Your Business*

"Tamra contributes to the growing chorus of those understanding the need to replace traditional performance appraisals. In addition to building on solid research in the social sciences, she recognizes the need to challenge an organization's culture and underlying beliefs about motivation, leading to tailored solutions for performance management. What sets this book apart from the others is the detailed collaborative design and implementation process using very effective visual tools and techniques. This book is a key resource for those committed to unleashing the full potential of their organization."
—Mary Jenkins, coauthor of *Abolishing Performance Appraisals* and founder of Jenkins People Systems

"If your company is straining under the weight of a performance management system that was created when Herbert Hoover was president and George VI was sitting on the throne of England, this book is for you. What sets this book apart is Tamra Chandler's practical, research-driven methodology to create something new and better that will actually stick in your organization because it enlists people in the design and reboot. Chandler's 'Eight Fundamental Shifts' and 'Three Common Goals' provide a great framework that treats everyone like adults and helps organizations achieve their strategic goals."
—Jane Takushi, Director, Talent Management, Apptio

"If you are starting on a journey to HR's future, read this book. At its deepest, it is an invitation to rethink how we practice HR. Bring trust, collaboration, and accountability into your culture; deliver feedback in forthright, timely conversations; fundamentally reboot your manager and employee relationships; and shift to the next-generation talent management. Tamra speaks for all of us who have toiled in the profession for years waiting for the big shift to happen. It is grounded in the present but clearly shows the way to the future."

—**Anna A. Tavis, Executive Editor,** *People + Strategy Journal*

"Tamra's messages are fresh and relatable to all leaders committed to maximizing the performance of their people. Rich with real-world examples and practical advice and infused with humor, this book is a quick read and well worth your time!"

—**Kim Cannon, Executive Vice President, Human Resources, TrueBlue Inc.**

"Tamra Chandler's book quite rightly highlights how broken performance management systems are but, more importantly, offers valuable best-practice solutions on how to fix them. Given the proven linkage between performance management and employee engagement, her prompting of a 'performance management reboot' is long overdue. This book is a really great read for both manager and employee."

—**Kevin Sheridan** *New York Times* **bestselling author of** *Building a Magnetic Culture*

"This book demystifies the complex journey of evolving performance management. Tamra contrasts traditional approaches with innovative possibilities. She provides a step-by-step guide considering each organization's unique goals and culture. This will be a go-to resource to reinvent our performance management system."

—**Kori Czasnojc, Director of Organizational Development, Raley's**

"This book goes beyond outlining why the traditional performance appraisal process is dysfunctional to describing what basic attributes of the culture and approach to employees have to change to fix it. A great book to give to leaders to get them moving on reform."

—**Peter Cappelli, George W. Taylor Professor of Management and Director, Center for Human Resources, Wharton School, University of Pennsylvania**

"Tamra shows us how conventional performance management is profoundly flawed and provides us with a pragmatic and comprehensive road map leading to and sustaining transformational change. Tamra intertwines points of view, examples, tools, and change management practices that will properly serve those who have the courage—and encouragement—to make this bold change. Her performance management mindset and principles center appropriately around performance, fairness, and development."

—**Bob Hargadon, Senior Vice President, Global Human Resources, Alere, Inc.**

"Tamra has created an amazing resource to help you get your organization moving again. She packed it with humor and frontline case examples that you can immediately put into action. It is a quick read and well worth your time. I will be sending copies to my kids and other people I really care about. I highly recommend it for anyone who wants to lead more effectively!"

—**Steve Player, coauthor of** *Future Ready* **and** *Beyond Performance Management*

How Performance Management Is Killing Performance

AND WHAT TO DO ABOUT IT

How Performance Management Is Killing Performance

AND WHAT TO DO ABOUT IT

RETHINK. REDESIGN. REBOOT.

M. Tamra Chandler

BK

Berrett–Koehler Publishers, Inc.
a BK Business book

Berrett-Koehler Publishers, Inc.
1333 Broadway, Suite 1000
Oakland, CA 94612-1921
Tel: (510) 817-2277   Fax: (510) 817-2278   www.bkconnection.com

Ordering Information

Quantity sales. Special discounts are available on quantity purchases by corporations, associations, and others. For details, contact the "Special Sales Department" at the Berrett-Koehler address above.

Individual sales. Berrett-Koehler publications are available through most bookstores. They can also be ordered directly from Berrett-Koehler: Tel: (800) 929-2929; Fax: (802) 864-7626; www.bkconnection.com

Orders for college textbook/course adoption use. Please contact Berrett-Koehler: Tel: (800) 929-2929; Fax: (802) 864-7626.

Orders by U.S. trade bookstores and wholesalers. Please contact Ingram Publisher Services, Tel: (800) 509-4887; Fax: (800) 838-1149; E-mail: customer.service@ingrampublisherservices.com; or visit www.ingrampublisherservices.com/Ordering for details about electronic ordering.

Berrett-Koehler and the BK logo are registered trademarks of Berrett-Koehler Publishers, Inc.

Printed in the United States of America

Berrett-Koehler books are printed on long-lasting acid-free paper. When it is available, we choose paper that has been manufactured by environmentally responsible processes. These may include using trees grown in sustainable forests, incorporating recycled paper, minimizing chlorine in bleaching, or recycling the energy produced at the paper mill.

Library of Congress Cataloging-in-Publication Data
Chandler, M. Tamra
How performance management is killing performance and what to do
        about it : rethink, redesign, reboot / by M. Tamra Chandler. —
First edition. | Oakland, CA : Berrett-Koehler
        Publishers, 2016.
Includes bibliographical references.
        ISBN 9781626566774 (hardcover)
    1. Performance—Management. 2. Organizational effectiveness.
    I. Chandler, M. Tamra II. Title.
HF5549.5.P35 C43 2016
658.3/12—dc23
                                                                        2015036435

First Edition
20 19 18 17 16   10 9 8 7 6 5 4 3 2 1 First Edition

Book production and design: Seventeenth Street Studios
Copyeditor: Elissa Rabellino
Indexer: Richard Evans/Infodex
Proofreader: Laurie Dunn
Cover designer: Dan Tesser / Studio Carnelian
Cartoon and Cover illustrations: Dillon Sturtevant
Additional illustrations: Valerie Winemiller, Seventeenth Street Studios

The PM Reboot; Rethink, Redesign, Reboot; and the PM Sketchbook are trademarks of PeopleFirm, LLC.

For Alabaster, my superpower

Contents

Foreword

PERFORMANCE MANAGEMENT FACES A MAJOR PARADOX.
On the one hand, employees and managers all recognize, and studies confirm, that it is the most loathed HR practice. Performance management feels like hazing to the employees being appraised and makes isolated Scrooges of the managers doing the appraisal. As a result, managers hide behind performance management processes meant to quantify and validate behavior. These bureaucratic processes further alienate employees from managers and become administrative folderol. People game the process, and performance management does not improve performance.

On the other hand, accountability matters. Not all employees perform well on all tasks; employees often have differentiated performance; and employees often judge themselves by their intent (which is often positive) more than by their outcomes (which may not be). Without accountability, employees don't perform as well. Few people wash their rental car before returning it, but many fill it up with gas because of obvious accountability. I have tried to lose weight without weighing in, and my good intentions were not realized without accountability. Without accountability, people are unlikely to change and improve performance.

So performance management faces a conundrum. Don't do any performance management, and accountability sloughs and performance lags; keep building complicated processes, and the process breaks and performance lags.

Tamra Chandler not only does a marvelous job depicting this performance management enigma, but she also offers some thoughtful alternatives. As a consultant, she has had the opportunity to observe many leading companies that have both succeeded and failed in performance management. Her writing is engaging with clever metaphors, pictures, and examples. She simplified the complex and is inside her reader's head, trying to rethink and retool performance management.

She starts with what is. Her eight fatal flaws (chapter 2) of traditional performance management will likely leave you nodding in agreement and realizing you are not alone, but also cringing with recognition that good intentions are not working.

She moves to what can be. Her eight shifts (chapter 3) provide a blueprint for moving forward. These shifts are fundamental assumptions about information and people that allow positive accountability to occur.

She then begins with the end in mind by identifying three goals of positive performance management (chapter 4): developing people, rewarding equitably, and driving organization performance. She builds her performance management retooling on this tripod and shows how it can enable a positive conversation.

With shifts and goals defined, she suggests a PM Reboot, where leaders come with assumptions of trust and customization. Trust implies building relationships between employees and managers, listening to each other, sharing decision making, and working together on common goals. Customization means adapting, not adopting, ideas according to the company, job, and individual. Rather than have rigid and standardized processes, work to tailor accountability solutions. She then offers specific performance management redesign solutions in five phases:

- Mobilize: Plan and invite participants to get started.

- Sketch: Align on how to move forward.

- Configure: Prepare a performance solution.

- Build: Adapt the solution.

- Implement: Plan, change, and act on the ideas.

For each of these five phases, she offers specific examples and tools that leaders can use.

What is particularly helpful about Tamra Chandler's work is that she acknowledges what most have realized: that performance management is less about the process (setting goals, ensuring standards, having consequences, providing feedback) and more about positive conversations built on relationships. But she goes beyond the superficial adage "have a positive conversation" to offer specific guidelines, tools, and words that might allow these productive conversations to occur. It feels like she is a genie on the shoulder of a manager who wants to help his or her employees improve through a positive and accountable conversation. She is not prescriptive about a process, but she is committed to building trust and customizing an approach to performance improvement. As appropriate, she weaves in research to validate her recommendations (e.g., Hofsted's workplace cultures). Through the cases she provides, it is obvious that she has had many of these coaching roles and helped well-intentioned managers find the balance between rigid processes and accountability abdication.

Another nice feature about her work is that the principles she proposes apply in both for-profit and not-for-profit settings. I can imagine that these principles could also be adapted to social groups, church settings, and even families, where the paradox of accountability also exists.

Her last chapter (10) is an excellent and valued addition. Many people know what to do but don't do it (e.g., eating healthy, being kind to strangers, listening more). By anticipating resistances and dealing with them in advance, managers can overcome what might go wrong. Her work parallels the seven disciplines of sustainability that we found in helping leaders sustain the changes they know they should make.

Is this book a panacea for the accountability paradox? Probably not. But it is far more helpful than trudging ahead with what is broken or abandoning all sense of accountability. It is particularly insightful on how to build a customized, trusting relationship through a positive conversation. Will employees like knowing how they are doing and what they need to do to improve? Probably not in many cases. Will leaders like being the bearer of bad news and holding up an accountability mirror? Probably not in many cases. But, by managers rethinking, redesigning, and rebooting performance management, accountability can lead to better-developed people, equitable rewards, and sustained organizational performance.

Dave Ulrich
Rensis Likert Professor of Business, University of Michigan
Partner, the RBL Group

Preface

**IS PERFORMANCE MANAGEMENT ACTUALLY *KILLING*
PERFORMANCE?** Seems a little melodramatic, doesn't it? I'll admit
that the book's title may be a little over the top, but the fact is, my own
personal experience and a great deal of research confirm that a process
that was designed to increase engagement and productivity is doing
just the opposite, and in a big way. My aim is to help you understand
how performance management really is killing performance, but more
important, to show you exactly what you can do about it.

In fact, this may be the first comprehensive how-to guide to designing
modern, customized performance solutions ever published. But,
although it is about performance management, don't get the wrong
impression. It's really about creating something revolutionary that
looks *nothing* like what we know today as performance management. So
let's say instead that it's about creating high-performing organizations,
promoting individual development, and building on the collective
capabilities of a team of people. In short, rethinking, redesigning,
and rebooting performance management in a way that recognizes the
uniqueness of your people and your organization.

Whether you're a human resources or talent management
professional, a business leader, or a fellow consultant, or you hail from
some other corner of the organizational landscape, you've come to
the right place. I wrote this book for you: that bold individual in any
organization, be it large, small, local, global, high-tech, or low-tech, who
decides it is high time to rethink and redesign his or her team's approach
to performance management. I aim to give you both the courage to get
started and a guide to leading your organization through a thoughtful
process to reboot performance management and build a solution that
matches your strategy, culture, and needs, as well as the promises you've
made to your employees.

But my book isn't just for *you*. It's also for your executive team, your business leaders, your managers, and your employees. Why? Because I want to help everyone who has an interest in this topic, or a role to play in the process, understand why our traditional approaches to performance management are not working, and how we can and should shift our thinking to create better experiences and outcomes for all involved.

Building this understanding is the core aim of the first section of the book, **Rethink,** which was written for anyone who is touched by performance management. **Redesign** is where the rubber meets the road: an unprecedented step-by-step guide to designing your own customized solution. Finally, there's the all-important **Reboot,** which provides tips and tricks for building and implementing your solution and making it stick. As an added bonus, you will find a Toolbox section with guides, worksheets, and other tools to aid you in the practical application of the PM Reboot process. Look for the Toolbox icon ⊗ for these items throughout.

If you are taking on the job of "lead architect" of your future performance management solution, this book will be an indispensable road map to getting where you want to go. Read through it once, and then return to it as you work through each of the design steps in part 2 for helpful tools, techniques, tips, and facilitation guides along the way.

I strongly encourage you to ask your business leaders and others who play a role in your performance management process to read the Rethink section in particular. Use it to start the conversation within your organization and engage your broader team in the rebooting process.

As you read, you'll notice that I have a bit of fun examining the pitfalls of traditional performance management from time to time, particularly in chapter 2, but make no mistake: I have nothing but respect and admiration for the talented and dedicated HR practitioners who have worked so hard and for so long to try to make performance management better. I'm on your team and probably have more in common with you than you know; after all, as a seasoned consultant and business leader myself, I've been in the trenches with you for decades. In fact, I built a very efficient and thoroughly traditional performance management solution in my role as the people leader at Hitachi Consulting. Been there, done that—which helped convince me that it was time to move beyond tradition and find ways to help free HR professionals from a process that's typically stressful and ineffective and a role that is too often negatively viewed by those they support.

There's no doubt in my mind that what's broken here is the system, not the people who are stuck in it. And I'm clearly not alone. In June 2015, I spoke on this subject to an audience of about 1,250 human resources professionals at the National Society for Human Resource Management (SHRM) Conference in Las Vegas. At the beginning of my presentation, I asked everyone in the audience who genuinely loved their performance management program to stand up.

And how many of those 1,250 people did? *Two.*

After my talk, a man approached me to let me know that the only reason he had stood up was that his company *didn't even have* a performance management program. It was a funny moment, but a little sad at the same time.

Now, how about you? Would you stand up for your current performance management solution? It would be understandable if your first reaction was to defend something that you and your team had invested hours, days, months, and maybe even years in building and improving. You've always had honorable intentions, and it is likely that over time you have improved your approach to make it more helpful, consistent, and trusted. Or you might think, "OK, I don't *love* our program, but there are elements of it that are not so bad, and there are even bits that are quite good." I'd expect that there are, and I hope that as you build something new, you don't throw those good parts away.

Use this book to help you rethink the not-so-good parts and to shift the role that HR plays in your organization's performance processes to something that's both more fun for you and your colleagues and more valued by those you support. Your HR team can move away from policing and overseeing what's likely to be a counterproductive, frustrating process to becoming designers of great tools and content for your managers and your people. Imagine freeing HR from inventorying completed reviews, arguing about rating scales, and hounding people to get their forms in, and instead trading those headaches for more time to teach, coach, and inspire the people within our organizations. Now *that* would be a reason to stand up.

In a sense, this book is my own way of standing up—for a new and better way of doing things, and for those who are struggling to create richer experiences for their people and more positive outcomes for their organizations. When I first decided to write it, I reached out to a wonderful network of authors and asked each of them to share their experiences in crafting, publishing, and marketing a book. This was unexplored territory for me, and their insights have been invaluable along the way.

One of these authors is Geoff Bellman. He and I passed a lovely late-winter afternoon chatting in his north Seattle living room overlooking Puget Sound, enjoying hot tea and the cookies I had brought in exchange for his time. We had been talking about writing for a while when Geoff asked me, "So, why this book?" I guess I still hadn't answered that question clearly for myself, so I fumbled a bit for a response. After a pause he said, "I find I write because I have to get these ideas out of my head. I have a compelling need to share them."

In that moment, Geoff had put words to what was driving me. For years I'd been observing the impact that our old thinking and philosophies were having on people across well-intentioned organizations. Further, I knew the frustration of HR leaders who were trying to find a better way. My personal passion for creating win-win solutions for people and organizations had evolved into an obsession. Like Geoff, I felt an unshakable urge to share my learnings, ideas, thinking, and approaches in hopes that they would help us move beyond tradition to something new and better. I felt compelled to reach those beyond my network and client base, because if enough of us have the courage and the tools to move forward—to Rethink, Redesign, and Reboot performance management—we can lead a sea change in how and why we work.

Part I

RETHINK.

If you do not change direction, you may end up where you are heading.

—Lao Tzu

Chapter 1
WELCOME TO THE PM REBOOT

IT SEEMS LIKE A MILLION YEARS AGO. In reality, it was 1985.

That was the year I took my first real job as a newly minted engineer at the age of twenty-two, working at the Boeing plant in Everett, Washington, in support of the 747 and 767 programs. I carpooled to work with a group of guys, leaving Seattle at 6:30 each morning to be sure that we were in our seats by 7:15. We all sat in a row of identical metal desks facing our manager's door. No one had a computer; all of our data was stored on enormous mainframes, and if you wanted a printout, there were only a few guys in the group who could run it for you. One of the few other women in my group was our dedicated secretary (yes, secretary, not assistant), who spent her days tapping away at an electric typewriter. Three older engineers sat in the row in front of me: one smoked cigarettes, another a pipe, and the third cigars. They had all the bases covered.

At lunchtime, we younger engineers headed to the cafeteria for our thirty-minute break, while the older guys played cards and ate sandwiches they'd brought from home. The workload was steady but never overwhelming, and our forty-hour week allowed us plenty of time to get everything done. (Like many Boeing employees of that era, we referred to the company as "the Lazy B.")

We all had a set number of vacation days and sick days. My pay would incrementally increase each year, and I never saw a bonus. No one thought to ask for flextime beyond maybe a thirty-minute swing in arrival and departure times. We wouldn't have dreamed of taking work home, much less taking any along on vacation.

Our meetings involved packing into a single conference room. To communicate across the company to other engineering or support teams, we drafted memos and had the secretary type them up. After a few rounds of editing, we'd send them off in interoffice mail envelopes, and then we'd wait a few days for a response to return in a similar envelope. Everyone followed the same procedures and processes, and most communications from leadership came via memo or the company newsletter.

At the time, I simply accepted the fact that this was the way things had always been done, and it never occurred to me that they wouldn't continue to be done this way forever. After three years, I left Boeing to get my MBA and embarked on a quarter of a century as a leader and consultant in strategy, operational performance, human resources, and people solutions. Looking back, my days at the Lazy B seem like the Dark Ages; the metal desks, the secretary with her electric typewriter, the desktop ashtrays, and the forty-hour workweek survive only in my memories. We've seen five presidential administrations since then, ridden out a couple of cycles of economic boom and bust, and witnessed the dawn of the digital age and a new millennium.

Everything has changed. Everything, that is, except performance management.

Technology has altered the landscape dramatically; we're always on and connected. Turnaround times have gone from days to minutes. We often have a diverse mix of generations and nationalities working for us under one global corporate umbrella, and the roles of women in the workplace have changed considerably from the days of all-male management at Boeing. Our modern culture of self-expression, particularly in today's predominantly millennial workforce, has bred an unprecedented desire for creativity, autonomy, and fulfillment in the workplace. Many employees have an expectation of instant feedback, frequent recognition, and a strong say in their career paths. Teamwork, technology, and long hours collaborating in coffee shops have replaced working alone at a desk in a cubicle or office. For many of us, *going to work* has evolved into *doing work*.

Yet our approach to performance management remains stuck in the world of Rolodexes and two-martini lunches. The fundamentals of how we assess, develop, and motivate talent have changed little from the roots of the practice in the post–World War II industrial boom.[1] At that time, bureaucracies sought to align common thinking across the layers of their organizations and began working to drive behavior and performance standards across large companies. Then the late 1950s saw the emergence of management by objectives (MBOs), a review-based process designed to make sure that employees and management agree on what specific objectives the employee needs to achieve to support the organization. Thus, performance management largely became a scorecard of an individual's accomplishments.

By the time I began my career at Boeing in the mid-1980s, MBOs had become the norm, and performance management as we know it today flourished. The roots of MBOs remain to this day a key element of most performance programs, and we continue to see its widespread use as a means to measure whether or not employees are meeting objectives. In fact, today we find usage rates of performance appraisals at 90 percent or higher worldwide, and more than 97 percent here in the United States.[2]

I've delved into the workings of many organizations throughout my career as a consultant, and their approaches to traditional performance management always look pretty much the same. They usually include an annual appraisal and review process, maybe with a midyear check-in. Most often, performance is managed in a standard way across all employees, or at least across employee classes. Employees are commonly asked to complete a self-assessment based on a set of goals they created the previous year. They may be given definitions of core or leadership competencies to consider or assess. It may lead to an individual development plan, and it almost always includes some form of manager rating. An increasing number of organizations now include some type of calibration event or talent review in which managers meet to compare notes on their teams. These meetings may be orchestrated to achieve a recommended distribution or forced rankings by group or team. When all is said and done, the outcome of the process drives compensation, promotion decisions, and other rewards—and, for the unlucky, performance improvement plans (PIPs).

I'm guessing that the description above sounds pretty familiar and fairly innocuous, right? So why is this process so hated? After all, the purpose is a noble one. According to the Society for Human Resource Management, performance management is meant to be an "organized method of monitoring results of work activities, collecting and evaluating performance to determine achievement of goals, and using performance information to make decisions, allocate resources, and communicate whether objectives are met."[3] There's nothing wrong with that. Then where does it go so wrong? Why is a system that's supposed to make us perform better and help our organizations excel something we see as a necessary evil at best? Why does this system evoke such universal negativity—more than any other corporate initiative short of mass layoffs? Why is performance management killing performance?

From a Murmur to a Roar

My quest to solve this paradox began several years ago when I received a call from the chief HR officer of a large family foundation just up the street from the PeopleFirm office here in Seattle, asking our firm to write a white paper on performance management. Their HR team was beginning a process to redesign the foundation's performance management program, and they wanted to inform, educate, and challenge their leaders on the subject. Being a scientifically oriented group, they were looking for data based on solid research that proved a correlation between performance programs and organizational performance.

I jumped at the chance. My experience working with other companies and designing a performance solution from scratch during my days leading Hitachi Consulting's people strategy had convinced me that it was time to take a fresh look. At the time, I was interested in dissecting the entire traditional process: from the intent and underlying assumptions to the tools, norms, and practices, and ultimately to the expected outcomes and resulting impacts. And so it began.

In those early days of my journey, many academics and thought leaders were already questioning the value of traditional performance management, but there were only quiet murmurs among the real practitioners—the people in the trenches of actual organizations. Since then, the challengers, the outspoken, the brave, and even now the bandwagon jumpers have escalated the conversation from a murmur to a roar. Our collective dissatisfaction has inspired countless newspaper and magazine articles, blog posts, webinars, and conversations at HR and management conferences. And as the volume has increased, more and more research has validated what many of us already suspected: the commonly practiced techniques and approaches for managing performance that have been used by most organizations around the world for decades simply aren't working.

I don't want to take too much of your time wading through the research that supports my views, but let me give you a few highlights. Sylvia Vorhauser summed it up well with the following damning points regarding traditional performance management:

- Everyone hates it—employees and managers alike.

- Nobody does it well—it's a skill that seemingly fails to be acquired despite exhaustive training efforts.

- It doesn't do what it was designed to do—i.e., increase performance.[4]

She's hardly alone in her condemnation. In a recent Reuters poll, four out of five US workers said they were dissatisfied with their job performance reviews.[5] In a survey of forty-eight thousand CEOs, managers, and employees, only 13 percent of managers and employees and a mere 6 percent of CEOs thought their year-end reviews were effective.[6] The latest Performance Management Survey, which collected data from more than one thousand HR professionals, found that when respondents were asked if their performance management process was seen as contributing to individual performance, 47 percent—yes, nearly half of them—said they weren't sure if their performance management processes made *any contribution at all* (those are my italics, but you can understand why).[7] Finally, according to the Corporate Executive Board (CEB), a management research group, surveys have found that 95 percent of managers are dissatisfied with their PM systems, and 90 percent of HR heads believe they do not yield accurate information.[8]

There is plenty more research out there, but you get the gist. This leaves us with this question: if performance management isn't performing as we all hope, what is it doing? Well, a recent *Psychology Today* article notes that at least 30 percent of performance reviews result in *decreased* employee performance.[9] Take a moment to ponder that: it's actually achieving the *opposite* of its original intent.

And yet we find that, despite all the talk and all the evidence that a change is needed, the majority of organizations have yet to *substantially* change their performance management approach. I'm talking about real action—what many might consider radical change. This doesn't mean just tweaking your ratings model from a five-point to a six-point scale. Instead, it means sitting down with a clean sheet of paper and starting over. It means asking yourself, "What outcomes are we seeking? What do our people need now and for their futures? How do we deliver on those needs in a simple and effective manner?"

You may have heard about those who were the first movers toward rethinking performance management for their unique organizations: Adobe, Kelly Services, Oakley, and others. We owe thanks to these trailblazers, and while we can learn from their experiences, what works for them may not be the right answer for all. What's important is that they actually *did* something to change the equation, and now we need to examine why we haven't made the same leap. If we know it is time for change, then what more do we need to spur us to action? What will it take to get the rest of us, the hesitant majority, to reboot?

After poring over the research and discussing the issue extensively with a lot of teams from a lot of companies, I've found that the top barriers to rebooting performance management are clear:

1. We can't get the executives there: there's too much resistance to moving away from what they've always known.

2. Managers get a "no confidence" vote: executives and HR practitioners alike lack trust in their managers to lead the performance process, and they're reluctant to give the managers authority on critical people-related decisions like pay and promotion.

3. Most are simply unsure how to fix it holistically, especially when you throw compensation into the mix. Too many are still asking, "What is the alternative? How do we get from where we are today to where we want to be?"

So my journey led me to the understanding that yes, there is a problem, and yes, we need to change, but the frustrating fact is that practical solutions have seemed to be out of reach of those looking for answers. Having spent a lifetime working with clients to translate research, know-how, and ideas into real, working business solutions, I took on the mission to solve the problem, to crack the code once and for all.

My goal for this book is to give you the tools to overcome the resistance of skeptical business leaders, as well as the insight and methods to help ready your managers and your people for when you hand them the keys to drive your organization and their own careers. Most important, my aim is also to arm you with a practical technique for successfully tackling this complicated problem, so that once you're ready and you're staring at that clean sheet of paper, you'll have a solid approach to breaking away from the old and starting something completely new. I call it **the PM Reboot**.

On one level, the PM Reboot is a design process to guide you step-by-step as you navigate the complex terrain of delivering on the goals of performance management. But dig deeper and you'll see that the PM Reboot is a philosophy—maybe even a revolution—that challenges common management beliefs and discards hackneyed and outdated techniques. The PM Reboot switches out musty assumptions that have led to narrow, standardized tactics for modern ideas that are rooted in science and that place people back at the center of any solution. At its core, the PM Reboot philosophy is grounded in two concepts: *trust* and *customization.*

TRUST: Top performance (and great employee experiences) are best achieved by letting go of control and trusting your people—which is, of course, easier said than done. Trust requires us to drop the oversight and tired formulas in favor of informing and empowering employees and managers. It allows us to set our sights on creating great careers, building on individual strengths, and celebrating the power of teams.

CUSTOMIZATION: Why should we expect Walmart's approach to performance management to be the same as Nordstrom's? We shouldn't. This is the second big idea that underpins the PM Reboot philosophy. Every organization is unique; therefore, every organization deserves a performance management solution that supports that uniqueness. Even discrete employee segments have attributes that can differ greatly from one another. And when you drill down to the individual level, we all know that each and every one of us is our own special snowflake. No two of us are alike, so what works well for one may not work for the other. Factor in these layers of uniqueness and individuality, and we are forced to realize that a one-size-fits-all approach to performance management from one enterprise, group, or even individual to another is probably doomed to failure.

In the chapters that follow, I'll share with you an illustrated guide to incorporating trust and customization into every aspect of your performance management solution. Together we will find the path to building high performance and employee engagement, while optimizing your performance management program for today's increasingly connected, volatile, and multigenerational business world.

At each step in designing your custom solution, I'll share proven frameworks, tools, and facilitation techniques as well as best practices on how to engage everyone in your organization—from the top executives to the newest employees—in order to build support and readiness. I'll also help you visualize the possibilities offered by the PM Reboot as it applies to four organization types based on real-life examples.

But first we need to rethink performance management by examining what's broken in the world of traditional programs and identifying the fundamental shifts that must be embraced when designing your custom performance solution.

Chapter 2
THE EIGHT FATAL FLAWS

I ASSUME YOU'VE PICKED UP THIS BOOK BECAUSE you're already convinced that traditional performance management is broken and you're looking for answers. But it's also possible that you're a skeptic, and you need more convincing that it's time to try something new. Then again, you may be reading this simply because you were asked, encouraged, or arm-twisted into giving it a go.

Whatever your perspective, this chapter is for you. If you're ready and willing to move on to something new, it will provide important context about the evils you're moving away from. If you're a skeptic, it will give you compelling data and insights from experts in the field that I hope will convince you that the old ways are not necessarily the best ways, and perhaps I'll manage to unstick a few of your assumptions and beliefs. What I ask is simply this: consider these flaws in light of your own personal experiences. I have yet to find anyone who can't relate to some, if not all, of the issues that arise from traditional methods of performance management.

In my years of immersing myself in this topic, I've read through the studies, research, and anecdotal evidence; I've explored perspectives from various angles; I've listened to my clients' experiences; and I've worked with companies as they set out to find something better. Through it all, I've come to the conclusion that there are eight basic reasons that our old standby performance management process creates such distrust, disengagement, and wasted effort. In other words, eight reasons why traditional performance management is almost universally hated.

I call them the Eight Fatal Flaws.

Fatal Flaw #1: A theory without evidence is just a (bad) theory. There is no evidence that traditional performance management leads to improved performance.

I think we can safely assume that a primary and expected outcome of the time, resources, and energy we invest in performance management is improved performance, both for individuals and for the organization. Yet I'm going to tell you straight out that there is no sound evidence that supports this idea. Reflect on the research findings I shared in the first chapter, and you can only conclude that science has found traditional performance management to be untrusted and ineffective, and that its contributions are dubious at best. In fact, its true and realized impact is often counterproductive and utterly at odds with its core purpose.

> *There is a mismatch between what science knows and what business does. . . . Too many organizations are making their decisions, their policies about talent and people, based on assumptions that are outdated, unexamined, and rooted more in folklore than in science.*[1]
>
> —DANIEL PINK, AUTHOR OF *DRIVE*,[2]
> IN HIS TED TALK "THE PUZZLE OF MOTIVATION"

Common sense, as well as a good deal of research, tells us that engaged people and teams make for higher-performing organizations. Recognizing this linkage, it seems reasonable to assume that if performance management led to higher levels of employee engagement, there would be little reason to change our way of doing things. But here the connection breaks down. Performance management as we know it is not increasing morale, and it's not driving engagement. If there were a clear connection, then logic dictates that we would see an increase in employee morale correlated with the expanded usage of conventional performance management. And we simply don't. In fact, the data shows that the process is far more effective at creating disengagement.

In the context of neuroscience research, most PM practices turn out to damage the performance they are intended to improve.
—DAVID ROCK, JOSH DAVIS, AND BETH JONES,
"KILL YOUR PERFORMANCE RATINGS"[3]

The brutal truth is, we've built old-school performance management on beliefs and assumptions about how to motivate and improve human performance that are faulty and that fail to deliver on their promise. Best intentions, wrong tactics. In the pursuit of recognizing differentiated performance, we've created unhealthy competition and opportunities to game the system. We've built standardized processes and policies in the pursuit of fairness, but what we've wound up with are mind-numbing tick-the-box exercises that minimize the human side of a process that is essentially all about people. Seeking to drive manager-employee communication, we've trained people to time-box conversations that should be sought openly by both parties and that should happen in the moment. Dialogue that should be ongoing is instead relegated to a prescribed place and time with a defined agenda that too often creates an adversarial or banal tone. In the interest of accountability, we encourage people to set specific and aligned goals, but too often this system rewards those who undercommit and play it safe.

See where I'm going here? There's no good reason to continue using techniques that have been shown scientifically to be unproductive or, in some cases, even counterproductive. It's time to make our good intentions stick by switching to methods that have been proven to increase engagement, which is the key to driving real and sustainable business performance.

Fatal Flaw #2: Nobody opens up with the person who pokes them in the eye. Traditional performance management impedes the reception of feedback and limits honest dialogue.

Imagine that you're an employee whose third child has just arrived. You really need just two things: more sleep and a raise. At your company, the possibility of that raise is tied to your yearly performance review, which is coming up in a few weeks. What do you do? You plan for that danged thing. You dredge up every last project you've completed and work to spin it so that you look golden. You collect evidence and forward it to your boss. You get yourself all amped up for the conversation ahead. You're pumped. You're going to kill it!

> *A performance appraisal is about believing that others hold the secret to your own worth.*
>
> —DICK RICHARDS, *ARTFUL WORK*[4]

Now let's freeze-frame and look at your state of mind at this point. Are you going to be open to hearing anything your supervisor might say that doesn't support your story? Are you in a mental place where you can take in and process feedback on your performance? No, you aren't. According to research by David Rock, an expert in leadership neuroscience,[5] when we receive a rating or appraisal, our brain shifts into "fight or flight" mode, which triggers our limbic brain. This shift—which happens whenever we feel threatened—immediately results in defensiveness. So the very act of executing a performance appraisal itself reduces performance.[6]

Your survival is at stake (or at least it feels like it is). Your focus is entirely on making yourself look good, on "winning" that performance review, and the last thing you're in the mood to talk about is where you need more development.

When we analyze this scenario, we can see that the inherent dynamics of the situation have moved you away from a positive outcome in three major ways:

1. The review has made your boss an adversary. Heaven forbid she doesn't agree with the rosy picture you've painted. Any whiff of disagreement between the two of you will only heighten the adversarial tension.

2. Your goal isn't to have a dialogue. You're thinking of it first as a sales job and then, if necessary, as a debate. You sure aren't going in to have a heart-to-heart or to admit to any weakness in front of her.

3. The situation has placed the control in the hands of your manager. This reinforces the superior-subordinate relationship—the opposite of empowerment.

And what is on this manager's mind? you ask. Well, let's put ourselves in her shoes for a moment. Imagine you have seven employees reporting to you. Your team has had a solid year, but you have extremely limited resources to offer salary increases (or any other perks, for that matter). Even worse, your executive leadership has made it clear that if you rank too many of your people as top performers, you'll be reviewed lower yourself for being too lenient and for violating "top performer" quotas. But there isn't a clear "low performer" in the bunch: each has contributed well, collaborated with one another, and ultimately delivered great results. As the manager, are you going to go into this conversation with an open mind and as a keen collaborator in your employee's success? Sadly, no. It's likely that you will be defensive from the get-go. How could you not? You're caught in a bind, denying rewards to employees you feel have earned them while defending a position and a process you don't agree with. Talk about demoralizing.

> *Most performance review systems reinforce a paternalistic world, one built on distrust and the assumption that the boss knows more about our skills, abilities, and commitment than we do. This dependency works against empowerment.*
> —RICK MAURER, *TOOLS FOR GIVING FEEDBACK*[7]

But what about the rest of the year, when the performance review isn't just around the corner? Isn't everyone inclined to be more open then? Unfortunately, no. The superior-subordinate paradigm set up by the performance review process creates a permanent barrier to open dialogue between managers and employees. As Professor Samuel Culbert notes in his book *Get Rid of the Performance Review!*, "The conversation between the boss and subordinate is forced into a box that undermines straight-talk interactions and colors every conversation between the two of them for the next 364 days."[8]

There is simply no way you as an employee can have an open and honest conversation about your own performance, hopes, fears, and goals with a person who is going to judge you, especially if her judgment affects such important aspects of your life as salary, recognition, and promotion. And that person who has to judge you? She's not going to have an honest conversation about how you can grow and develop if she knows that she has to keep your expectations low, or dash them altogether, often for reasons that have nothing to do with the quality of your performance.

The result? Open communication doesn't stand a chance.

Fatal Flaw #3: Nobody remembers the good work.

Performance reviews generally emphasize the negative, rather than focusing on strengths.

If you have any doubt that people tend to fixate on negative events and experiences, just take a look at the nightly hit parade of shootings, fires, and high-speed chases on the local news. This same tendency may explain why it feels much more natural for a manager to think about what an employee has done wrong than to focus on how to build on his strengths. That project he stubbed his toe on, the one that required you to step in and clean things up, delaying launch by a week? You never seem to totally forget that. The fact that he's a really good natural negotiator and might be trained to use that skill to contribute to the company's bottom line? That might easily get lost in the shuffle.

> *Humans are hard-wired to focus on the negative, so balanced feedback always leaves us concentrating on the bad parts.*
> —PETER CAPPELLI, WHARTON CENTER
> FOR HUMAN RESOURCES [9]

Author and business consultant Marcus Buckingham has conducted extensive research on performance and how it relates to an individual's strengths. He's found that only 25 percent of employees say their supervisors discuss their strengths at all in performance conversations.[10] And we wonder why employees tend to loathe this process.

Let's look at it from the employee's point of view. Let's say "Employee You" goes to a professional photographer. Fifty or sixty pictures are taken. Some are great, some are lousy. You pick your favorite and bring it with you into your manager's office. You present the picture and say, "This is me. I'm looking pretty good, don't you think?" Your manager brings out another picture, one that was taken when you were eating a chili dog in the cafeteria. Your mouth is open and a big blob of chili sauce is running down your shirt. Your manager says, "I think this is a more accurate picture of you."

And this, in essence, is what the annual review process feels like to a lot of people. They head into the session feeling pretty good about their performance over the past year, only to find out that their manager (who in many cases hadn't talked to them much throughout the year) has a different view. And sure, the image their manager holds may be only one negative event or instance, but it's heavily influenced the way he thinks of you and is likely to influence his approach to your annual review and to the downstream decisions of ratings, advancements, and project assignments. I'm not talking just about bad managers here; even the good eggs can fall into this trap. But how?

First, we commonly apply a strategy that assumes feedback is a motivator. News flash: it is not, for anyone. Researchers have found that even those who are inclined to seek learning opportunities don't like feedback—they may just dislike it a little less than others.[11]

Then there's the fact that differing expectations and sensitivities can undermine real communication. Even when we mean to be complementary, we may send signals that are interpreted negatively by the receiving individual. Expressing something as simple as "You were the second-highest-rated person in the company" may seem like a worthy compliment to the manager, but the employee may be thinking, "How can I not be number one?"

Finally, the system itself can get in the way. When operating within a forced distribution system or ranking system, managers may tend to focus more on justifying their assessments than on engaging in a healthy career-oriented conversation that looks to the future and engages the employee in what could be rather than what has been.

> *The more our value feels at risk, the more preoccupied we become with defending and restoring it, and the less value we're capable of creating in the world.*
> —TONY SCHWARTZ, *HARVARD BUSINESS REVIEW*[12]

Fatal Flaw #4: No man (or woman) is an island. The focus is on the individual, even though system or organizational challenges often have a significant influence on individual performance.

Let's tell another story here about Employee You. Suppose you're in product development. At the end of last year, the organization put in a new system of checks and balances in order to provide better quality control of the end product. These checks and balances take a lot of your time, so your productivity has plummeted. Then there's the additional rigor concerning product design that's inhibited some of your usual out-of-the box creativity. But your end products comply much better with the company standard, and you've created some solid sellers. So how does your manager respond to this mixed bag of results? How can he separate out what's in your control (and therefore fair game for discussion) and what's not? The answer is that he can't.

> *If we cannot segregate the impact of the system or the situation in assessing an individual's performance, we need a new theory.*
>
> —TOM COENS AND MARY JENKINS,
> ABOLISHING PERFORMANCE APPRAISALS[13]

Unfortunately, performance management is currently designed to focus on the performance of the individual and only the individual. This assumes, first, that improving the performance of each individual will drive an aggregate improvement of the organization (which is not necessarily the case), and second, that reviewers can discern the difference between the impact that a situation has on an individual's performance and the actual work of the individual being reviewed. Needless to say, this is a nearly impossible task.

Current research shows that the system (how work gets done in your company) actually has more influence than the individual can ever hope to have on the performance of both the individual and the organization as a whole. A recent Harvard study showed that only 46 percent of the sampled investment analysts were able to reproduce their performance in a new company, despite the fact that all of them were star performers at their previous banks.[14] One reason? According to the study, "The success of individual star performers is rarely the result of raw talent alone but also builds on the *support structure around them*" (italics mine). In other words, the situation, the environment, and the surrounding team are a large part of what makes a star performer. This means that your company might gain greater benefit by focusing on improving the system than by trying to improve the individuals who make up that system.

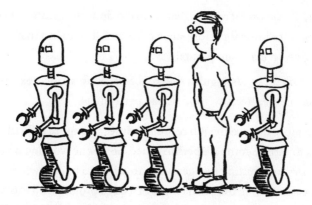

Fatal Flaw #5: We are not machines. Fairness and standardization in ratings and the judgment of performance simply cannot be achieved.

We are all human. Even the best and brightest among us are astonishingly fallible. Unfortunately, the traditional system relies heavily on the concept of an impartial, omniscient individual who can, without bias, unfailingly assess human output across a variety of roles and occupations. It's a stretch to assume that even one such person exists, much less to expect that every manager possesses that kind of objectivity and wisdom. And it's especially ridiculous when it comes to stack-ranking systems, or systems that require number ratings. I've seen rating systems that extend to two decimal places. Two decimal places?! Who in their right mind really thinks they can tell the different between a 4.35 performer and a 4.36? Yet in traditional performance management systems, advancement and salary decisions may very well rest on such infinitesimal and arbitrary distinctions. It's ludicrous.

> *An objective performance review is an exercise in self-delusion, the fantasy created by bosses who are convinced that they can somehow rise above the biases that make us all humans.*
>
> —SAMUEL CULBERT AND LAWRENCE ROUT,
> *GET RID OF THE PERFORMANCE REVIEW!*[15]

In fact, it's the use of ratings that seems to draw the greatest ire from the critics of traditional performance programs. I've found that most tend to agree on five main points:

1. It's difficult to distinguish differences in performance, except in the case of exceptionally good or bad performers.

2. The more diverse the job responsibilities, the more difficult it is to rate or compare performance. Someone working on a factory line putting two gee-gaws together to build a widget is a lot easier to rate than a manager of a large project with multiple responsibility areas. Then there's the case of people with jobs that might look similar on paper (say, two management positions), but could nonetheless involve dealing with vastly different projects, stakeholders, geographies, vendor partners, or technology platforms.

3. People will attempt to fix the results by manipulating and distorting ratings to get to a desired number.

4. There is a whole host of biases, prejudices, and personal quirks that influence a person's appraisal of others. Research shows that approximately 60 percent of any given performance rating actually has to do with the traits of the person conducting the evaluation and not the person being rated, a phenomenon known as "the idiosyncratic rater effect."[16] While we think our ratings are telling us something about the ratee, they're actually revealing far more about the rater.

5. Even for those raters who are trying their best to remain unbiased and fair, it's almost impossible to remember the whole year with equal acuity. It's only human to put more weight on an event, whether it's positive or negative, that happened just last month than on one that took place almost a year ago.

By expecting one human to assess another in a system that borders on the robotic, we fail to take our essential nature as humans into account, both our strengths and our shortcomings. We are not machines, so why have we become so resigned to assessing human performance in such a mechanical way?

Fatal Flaw #6: We are not machines, redux. Review output is unreliable for making talent decisions.

So if it's virtually impossible for managers to make fair, unbiased judgments on the performance of their employees, why do these reviewer inaccuracies err so often on the side of leniency? Believe it or not, 90 percent or more of those reviewed end up in the Meets, Exceeds, or Significantly Exceeds category.[17] In short, managers tend "to be more 'nice' than 'accurate.'"[18]

I've been telling you how demoralizing reviews are, and I've been saying how we all tend to focus on the negative, and now I tell you that most people are actually getting scored higher than they should? Does that even make sense? Well, let me explain. When it comes to scoring people—giving people a rating that's going to be documented in their employee record—we generally tend to be more lenient than accurate (unless we have to stack-rank people, but that's another story). However, when it comes to talking to people and trying to give them feedback, human nature leads us to focus on those areas we see as weaknesses—

for the simple reason that we see them as the areas that need the most improvement. If you think about it, we're simply having a breakdown of coaching skills; without some training in what to do instead, most of us genuinely don't know how else to help people. Or we've been raised to believe that negative feedback is the way you make people grow (the performance management version of "spare the rod, spoil the child"). So the result is that, in person, we tend toward more harsh assessments of performance, but when rating, we tend toward more generous assessments.

So here's the problem: performance management scores traditionally supply the data for all sorts of important business functions, such as compensation management, succession planning, development goals, and employee performance reporting. If the data is inaccurate, then you're making business decisions based on faulty foundations, and your ability to make the best choices about investments in your workforce and organization is limited. The problem is that you still have to make these decisions, whether it's with good data or not. But does that mean that traditional performance programs (the ones that are just spitting out numbers) are your only option, even though they're actually getting in the way of good decisions? No, they're not.

How about if we tried allowing people to make these complex decisions in a manner that didn't come down to a figure in a box or a number based on something as ridiculous as how an employee was measured on the ambiguous value of "integrity"? I can tell you that just about every one of my clients is seeking to drive more differentiated recognition, and most are failing because the current process is limiting their ability to make better decisions. This process is used by humans and for humans; and for all our faults, it's actually good to be human—to ponder complexities, seek other people's input, and make thoughtful decisions. If we want better outcomes, we must move away from designing systems that attempt to eliminate our humanity from the equation and relieve leaders from making tough talent decisions. Simply put, any performance management system that is designed without people at its heart is doomed to failure no matter how many times you try to reboot it.

Fatal Flaw #7: Let me introduce you to your competition—now play nice together! Comparing people against one another erodes efforts to create a collaborative culture.

Imagine you're competing with your coworkers for a limited number of salary increases and promotions—or worse, just to keep your job (yes, some companies infamously let the bottom-ranked people go every year). Now imagine that the main factor in that competition is your yearly review score. Perhaps your company uses a five-point scale, and anyone below a four is unlikely to see an increase or advancement. Maybe your company falls into that grim group of stack rankers, so you'll soon be given your annual ranking against your peers. When the stakes are this high and the means of assessment are so arbitrary, it's the rare person who is indifferent. Most fall into one of two groups: those who resolve to claw their way to the top and those who resort to curling up into a metaphorical fetal position.

> *It makes no sense to talk of team- and partnership-oriented cultures, which our marketplace is now demanding, and still hold on to this artifact called performance appraisal.*
> —PETER BLOCK, IN FOREWORD TO
> *ABOLISHING PERFORMANCE APPRAISALS*[19]

Let's think about it. As a manager, are you going to inspire these two groups of people to give you their very best? Well, obviously, the people who are petrified instead of motivated by the process won't perform to their full potential. In his book *Punished by Rewards,* Alfie Kohn summarizes this better than I possibly could: "Competition creates anxiety of a type and level that typically interferes with performance. . . . Those who believe they don't have a chance of winning are discouraged from making an effort; having been given no reason to apply themselves except to defeat their peers, and convinced that they cannot do so, these people are almost by definition de-motivated."[20] Well said, Mr. Kohn.

"But," you say, "I don't want those people, anyway. I want people who throw everything into the work they are doing, like the competitive people. I'll bet they work hard." Well, yes, the people who are trying to claw their way to the top are going to work their tails off, or at least make it look like they are, but at the cost of their fellow team members. Remember, it's rare to get really great business results from employees working in a politically charged environment. It's pretty well established at this point that teamwork, communication, and collaboration are necessary ingredients to achieving real business success. Some may say that it's a dog-eat-dog world—maybe so. But I'm challenging you to consider that the methods dictated by traditional performance management define cultural norms more than we might care to admit. If we truly want creative, agile organizations in which people with diverse skills and backgrounds and perspectives can collaborate and are willing to take risks, then we must dismantle the competitive constructs that erode those ideals.

Fatal Flaw #8: We are not Pavlov's dog. Pay for performance does not deliver improved performance.

What gets you motivated on a rainy Monday morning in the middle of February? Do you push harder on your project to have a chance of making a bit more money next year? I doubt it. Sure, you'd like the raise (money is nice; nobody turns down a raise), but aside from a hot cup of coffee, what is really going to get you digging into your inner reserves on that cold morning and hunkering down to excel is the fact that your work fulfills you and you feel it's important.

Traditional performance management is based on the assumption that extrinsic motivators (those things you do to avoid punishment or get a reward) are the best way to get employees to work harder and better. But we know now that people are much more motivated by intrinsic rewards and that they work harder and better when they are doing things they find personally rewarding.[21]

In the corporate world, this translates into things like enjoying the work itself, feeling like a valued part of the team, or being motivated by the company mission. It doesn't translate into worrying about getting a bad review or whether or not you're going to get a 3 percent raise—at least not for sustained periods. People don't hold performance hostage to rewards.

In his extensive research, Alfie Kohn concluded that "no controlled study has ever found long-term enhancement in the quality of people's work as a result of any kind of rewards or incentive program."[22] A study by the American Compensation Journal conceded that financial incentives don't improve performance quality; contrary to popular thought, money just isn't the greatest motivator. (In fact, when it's perceived as being unfairly distributed, money is a great de-motivator).[23] Furthermore, studies show that for people with satisfactory salaries, nonfinancial rewards are more effective than extra cash in building long-term employee engagement across sectors, job functions, and business contexts.[24]

Extrinsic motivators are a poor substitute for the satisfaction derived from doing good work you're genuinely interested in. So maybe, rather than letting budget constraints define the limits of our rewards program, we should unleash the potential of our people by rewarding them with more opportunities to love what they are doing.

Houston, We Have a Problem

When only 6 percent of CEOs feel that their annual performance reviews improve organizational performance,[25] we know that traditional performance management isn't working, and we have a pretty good idea why. The inherent system is broken, having been built upon unfounded, archaic, and poorly conceived assumptions—the Eight Fatal Flaws.

I can't think of a better voice to sum it up than that of W. Edwards Deming. In his book *Out of Crisis,* he pulls no punches:

> *[The annual review] nourishes short-term performance, annihilates long-term planning, builds fear, demolishes teamwork, nourishes rivalry and politics. . . . It leaves people bitter, crushed, bruised, battered, desolate, despondent, dejected, feeling inferior, some even depressed, unfit for work for weeks after receipt of rating, unable to comprehend why they are inferior. It is unfair, as it ascribes to people in a group difference that may be caused totally by the system they work in.*
>
> —W. EDWARDS DEMING[26]

Chapter 3

THE EIGHT FUNDAMENTAL SHIFTS

SO WE HAVE A CHALLENGE BEFORE US: to move beyond our comfort zone, away from what we've known and what we've always done, and embrace our changed world—informed by what science, experience, and research tell us about building healthy organizations.

How do we let go of these archaic traditional practices and tap into the power of our people in today's increasingly connected, customizable, and millennial-driven business world? How do we create culture, structure, leaders, and processes that fuel our companies to outperform the competition?

> *The difficulty lies, not in the new ideas, but in escaping from the old ones.*
>
> —JOHN MAYNARD KEYNES, *THE GENERAL THEORY OF EMPLOYMENT, INTEREST, AND MONEY*[1]

In order to create an agile, involved, and dedicated workforce, we must shift how we've been taught to look at our people. And our people must shift their own habits and views on the role they play in their personal development and careers. We're going to have to apply some new thinking that doesn't come naturally to those of us who have been working in the business world for, ahem, a few years—thinking that often totally contradicts the way in which most of us have been taught to manage.

There are eight "shake-the-kaleidoscope" changes in perspective that you're going to have to embrace in order to create a high-performing organization in this day and age. They are the givens that should be baked into every aspect of your new performance management cake.

I call them the Eight Fundamental Shifts. Drumroll, please . . .

Fundamental Shift #1: Open the door.

Shift from: Need to know
Shift to: Transparency

If you want your employees to trust you, if you want them to feel connected to your mission, and if you want them to be able to react in an agile manner to changes in your business environment, then you have to get rid of the secrets. The closed-door meetings, the "for your eyes only" communications, the hush-hush salaries, the stealth-mode ratings—all of them. I know that secrecy is so ingrained in the way we do business that we can scarcely imagine a world without it. But have you thought about what you really gain by all that cloak-and-dagger stuff?

"Hey," you might protest, "we don't have a lot of secrets here—you must be talking about the other guys!" And you may honestly believe that, because you're not intentionally keeping your people in the dark about anything. You've tried to maintain a transparent corporate culture, but is it really as transparent as you think it is? Ask yourself these questions:

"Can members of my team easily explain the performance processes?"

"Can they confidently describe the connection between performance and pay?"

"Do they understand how their past performance assessments were established?"

"Do they know where they stand, and what they need to do to get to that next role?"

Chances are you can't honestly answer "yes" to all or even most of them. And the problem with your employees not fully understanding the workings of your performance management system is simply this: where there's no transparency, there's no trust.

Let me tell you about a company I know that has a highly over-engineered performance management process. The program includes four sections, each with its own rating approach. Each employee receives four different ratings. That's bad enough, right? But it gets worse. One of the four rated sections—how the individual's future potential is assessed within the organization—is never shared with employees, although it is included in their weighted overall score. Seriously. What an uncomfortable conversation that must be for each participant in the process, manager and employee alike.

How on earth can you have an authentic and open conversation when one of the basic tenets of the approach is that certain elements must be kept secret? How does keeping the review process secret and popping out a number at the end improve performance? How the heck do employees know what they need to do to improve if they don't know how that number was reached? And even more important, how are employees going to feel that they matter—that they are a trusted, mature member of the team? Restricting access to information, especially about something as critically important as an employee's own performance, is nothing more than a crude way of reinforcing that master-subordinate relationship that stifles motivation and communication.

Here's the deal: in order to react quickly to change, to be able to self-direct, and to feel a commitment to the greater good, employees need to know what's going on. They need to know what the organization as a whole is thinking. They need to be in the loop on how their performance fits in with everything around them, and how well they are stacking up to expectations and why. They need to feel that they are a valued part of this great, inspiring thing you call your company. And you can't keep secrets and still expect your employees to bond with your organization—you just can't.

Transparency shouldn't end at personal performance, either. Include the other elements that are clustered with most performance programs. I'm thinking of things like how the process works, what it takes to get a promotion, and how compensation is determined. You need to shift more of the power to your people—and we all know that knowledge is power. A 2013 *Talent Management* article thoughtfully noted, "To think the employment relationship was forever going to be healthy and good with one side having all the power and information—that was a flawed thought."[2] I couldn't agree more.

Supreme Court Justice Louis Brandeis famously observed, "Sunlight is said to be the best of disinfectants,"[3] and he was right. Informed employees make better decisions, and frankly, transparency helps keep leaders and decision makers in check. And the truth is, keeping secrets is nearly impossible in today's connected world anyway. We can go on GlassDoor and learn all about most organizations' salary bands by level, read about their hiring practices, and tune in to the reviews voluntarily provided by company employees. Perhaps we should be thinking about what information we want to be sure our employees receive from us rather than from alternative sources. Let's open the door and give our people the knowledge, information, and insight they want and deserve!

Fundamental Shift #2: Give the steering wheel to your employees.

Shift from: Management-driven
Shift to: Employee-powered

We can all agree that we need to treat employees like adults. But what does that mean? Well, adults know how and when they work best, and they'll do so because they want to succeed. Your best people don't want you to tell them how to do their jobs. Instead, they are looking for you to tell them where the organization is going and why. (And that destination had better be enticing, so that those top performers say, "Hey, I want to be part of that!") They need you to give them the tools, information, and knowledge to make the best choices and decisions on behalf of the organization. One of your jobs as a leader is to build the framework and culture that allows your people to operate at their peak potential. Put programs in place that empower employees to be successful at their jobs. Then, stand back and let them go. Share your strategy freely—the "what" you're trying to do—so that employees can figure out their own "how" to get there. When employees understand the trust you're placing in them by allowing them to engineer their own work life and daily functions, they will be more committed and more engaged, and they'll contribute far more.

What does this mean in performance management terms? It means ditching the scheduled top-down review. Instead, set the expectation that employees should ask for insights, coaching, resources, and, yes, feedback when they want it and need it—in other words, when it feels right to them. Managers need to make it clear that they are there to provide advice and support, and that they will make themselves available on the employee's timeline. As we've discussed, it's highly unlikely that any employee will walk into a yearly performance review in the proper frame of mind to hear and process feedback. But change that review process into a conversation that takes place on the employee's instigation—when the employee honestly *wants* to hear how he or she is doing and talk about the future—and you're going to have a far richer conversation, and a healthier interaction going forward.

Further, if managers shift their approach to one that builds a collaborative, two-way relationship with their employees, one anchored in frequent informal check-ins to ask how things are going and how they can help, the whole nature of the employee-supervisor relationship will evolve. My colleague Susan Scott at Fierce likes to say, "The conversation is the relationship."[4] So true, and when a commitment to informal check-ins becomes a habit, manager-employee relationships are likely to thrive as a result of the ongoing conversation that is created.

And what is the outcome of these healthy relationships? Employees are more comfortable asking for input, and they believe that their manager truly cares about their career and growth. Trusted managers will find that they have far more opportunities to provide helpful and welcome guidance.

So what about that person who never wants any feedback? Well, what about him? If there is a problem, address it. If he's just heads down on his work, chugging away perfectly happily and getting stuff done, why should we feel the need to interrupt his flow? I know it's a hard concept to grasp for many of us, and I'm not suggesting that you let managers off the hook. Quite the contrary: they need to be present and engaged, and provide in-the-moment coaching when necessary.

Shifting to these approaches will build trusted relationships between manager and employee, and in the long run it will have a greater impact than today's formally orchestrated annual review meeting. After all, the point here is to drive performance and improve engagement. No matter how this plays out for each individual, the key is to give ownership of the process to your employees.

Now let's take an even broader view of this idea and talk about putting *career ownership* in the hands of your employees. Whoa! Am I suggesting that they should decide when they get a promotion? No, nothing so radical. But why do we decide that Employee X would be great in Role Y and start to groom that person for that position without so much as looping him in on the plan? Yes, he might be an awesome customer service agent, but his heart is never going to be with your company if you keep him in customer service his whole life (even as a manager), if what he really yearns to do is product development. Instead, try empowering your people to shape the careers they want. Create role definitions with clear competencies associated with them. Make them public. Be transparent about what roles are available in the company, and what experiences and education that employees need to have to be considered for them. You can go further and provide transparency into what salaries are associated with each role to give employees the necessary information to make career decisions for themselves. Then talk to your people about which of those roles they want to aim for, and provide support to get them there, from training opportunities to real-world experience in the right areas. Help them to create the career that they want, not just the career that is easiest or best for you as their employer.

> *Human beings have an innate inner drive to be autonomous, self-determined, and connected to one another. And when that drive is liberated, people achieve more and live richer lives.*
> —DANIEL H. PINK, *DRIVE: THE SURPRISING TRUTH ABOUT WHAT MOTIVATES US*[5]

At PeopleFirm, we've created the Lily Pad Career Development Model. Each of the roles in our company has its own "lily pad" with a clear role definition and the necessary competencies to rock that role. Each Tribe member can then "hop" from lily pad to lily pad as his or her ambitions, interests, and work experience change and mature. Ultimately our Tribe members decide when they want to move to that new role. The firm obviously must have a business need for that role, but this at least allows us to put our employees in the driver's seat of their own careers as much as possible.

A career program of this nature isn't just a pretty idea. It's also built on the science of what drives true employee engagement. Take, for example, the data in Mercer's 2013 *What's Working* study that found that "the *work itself,* including opportunities for development" (italics mine), was primary in driving engagement.[6] Daniel Pink has ingrained into many of us the idea that "mastery, autonomy, and purpose"[7] are the prime motivations that drive us as humans, and a recent Executive Conference Board found that involvement in job decisions has an exponential impact on employees' satisfaction in the work they are doing.[8] It's the nature of satisfying work, and the opportunity to have a say in what that work is, that are the key drivers of engagement.

The interesting hitch in all this is the challenge of getting employees to understand that they (rather than their supervisor, their manager, or HR) own their careers. The organization owns the responsibility of providing as much transparency, content, tools, and support as it can muster to help employees achieve the goals they are seeking. But because most of us have grown up being *told* instead of *asked,* employees often can't quite believe that the steering wheel is now in their hands. Getting comfortable with the idea of taking this ownership leap might require concentrated effort. Initially, employees may need to be reminded repeatedly that *they own it.* If you hear someone complaining that she's not getting any feedback, your first question should be, "Did you ask for it?"

Fundamental Shift #3: Change your focus.
Shift from: Focus on past performance
Shift to: Focus on future capability

The core of performance management programs has long been the performance review, which means we spend a majority of our time looking back at things that happened in the past. And this means we don't spend nearly enough of our time considering the future. When we look back, we tend to focus more on the negative than the positive. Nobody but a saint can sit through a litany of his past errors (or "opportunities for improvement") without developing a hefty case of defensiveness. And defensiveness begets deafness. We all know this at some level; if you've ever had a review discussion about someone's past error, you can probably pinpoint the moment his expression told you that he'd simply shut down. It's how we're wired: there is absolutely nobody on this earth who likes criticism, no matter how good they might seem to be at taking it.

But what if you want to tell someone that he did all sorts of wonderful things during the past year? Shouldn't you bring those things up? Well, yes. But ideally that should have happened when he actually *did* them (remember, real-time discussions are the aim). Talking about great stuff he did in the past makes for an enjoyable little ego massage, but it doesn't propel you forward. What does propel you forward is talking about how those great things are the foundation for his next step in the organization and reminding him that you're there to help him think about the next bricks he's going to lay on that foundation as he builds the career he's seeking.

Samuel Culbert is a big fan of turning the focus to the future. In his book *Get Rid of the Performance Review!*, he coins the phrase "performance *preview.*" Performance previews are "problem-solving . . . discussions about how we, as teammates, are going to work together even more effectively and efficiently than we've done in the past. . . . *The preview structure keeps the focus on the future* and what 'I' need from you as 'teammate and partner' in getting accomplished what we both want to see happen" (italics mine).[9] The performance preview aligns nicely with the other ideas we've been talking about, as it hands the employee the keys to his career and pulls the manager, supervisor, and surrounding employees into the care team that supports his career growth.

On the face of it, this shift is pretty basic. Instead of emphasizing what employees did or didn't do this last year, take time to focus on what they could achieve in the future, especially with support from you and the organization as a whole. Look at their strengths, capabilities, and skills, and talk about how to build on them. Explore what their interests are, the experiences they are seeking, and the roles or future positions they'd like to hold. Discuss how they can get there and what they need to do to start the process. Ask what help they need—what you or others can do to help them make their aspirations real. Listen to them, challenge them, and be their partner in building their future.

The part that is not so basic (and will, in fact, take a lot of practice) is having the insight and information to engage in a rich conversation with an employee about his or her future. For instance, you'll need to have a clear handle on the roles available within the organization and the expectations of those roles. As an organization, you'll need to make career paths transparent. Optimally, this career information should be readily available to employees so that they can come to their career conversations informed about their options and aware of the potential opportunities and challenges ahead of them. As HR departments, talent managers, and organizational development professionals shift their focus from overseeing and policing performance programs, my hope is that they'll devote that newfound bandwidth to building this career and role insight. Wouldn't creating career and development clarity be far more fun and rewarding than tracking down overdue performance reviews?

Another challenging element for many leaders is being willing to encourage career advancement choices that are good for your employee but may not be best for your team or group, at least not in the short term. Often it's our best performers who want to move on to new challenges, and those new challenges may very well lie in other departments. In these cases, it's important to remember that one of the top drivers of retention is the belief that the organization truly values its employees. Helping them take that fulfilling next step—even (or especially) if it means away from your group—is an incredibly powerful way of showing how much you value them. It's far better for them to leave your team for another one within the company than to leave the organization, full stop.

> *One reason talented people leave is because their manager hoarded them. You may have to let them go to let them grow. You might lose them from your team but save them for the enterprise!*
>
> —BEVERLY KAY AND SHARON JORDAN-EVANS,
> *LOVE 'EM OR LOSE 'EM*[10]

Fundamental Shift #4: Abandon uniformity.
Shift from: One size fits all
Shift to: Customized and nuanced

Have you ever looked at your performance management processes and policies through the lens of how they affect your employees? Have you set aside the question of what they are trying to achieve and focused instead on how well they support different individuals and groups throughout the company? You probably haven't, and why should you? Our corporate default tends to be a one-size-fits-all approach. Most companies simply never think to look at how well those policies mesh with the various locations, focuses, backgrounds, skill sets, career stages, and role needs of their employees.

We are in an era that is obsessed with efficiency and effectiveness, so we have been scaling our processes globally, seeking quality, consistency, lower costs, and improved returns through the elimination of duplicate efforts and the establishment of common practices. The mantra for many organizations has been "Streamline, optimize, and standardize." So it makes total sense that we'd build one common standardized solution for performance and roll that out across our organizations with little concern for borders, employee types, or cultural differences.

Here's the shift I'm proposing: What if we *did* look at our performance management processes with the users in mind? What if, instead of blanketing entire organizations with the same solution, we built more flexible systems that allowed our people to choose what worked for them, either as an individual (when appropriate) or as a work group inside the organization? Imagine the power of an organization that builds programs differently for groups or individuals with unique needs, so that those programs and policies accurately reflect the requirements, maturity, location, and desires of the people they support. Instead of a performance management system that says, "Here's how you need to do this," imagine one that allows each team, department, business unit, job family, or individual to configure its own customized approach.

Need an example? What I am talking about is allowing your sales team in California to handle performance management differently than your software developers in Pakistan or your factory workers in Vermont. When I put it that way, it seems painfully obvious, right? Those disparate employee groups have practically nothing in common, and treating them as if they do makes no sense and often has negative performance effects, not to mention the bureaucratic hassle of forcing people to comply with programs that don't work for them. Move away from the cut-and-paste bureaucracy with standard, vanilla rules and you can pride yourself on being a company that shows its employees that their individual needs and styles matter.

OK, I get how this might send a chill through your bones if you're an HR or business leader. How on earth are you supposed to manage a large organization in which each entity has its own custom approach? How can you control all that? Well, what if you tried not controlling all that? Instead, what about offering a menu of options from which groups or individuals within the enterprise can choose? Those options should be rooted in what performance means to your organization and some common principles for how you want to manage to that goal. For this nuanced approach to work, you'll need to be absolutely sure that you're starting with a solid foundation that makes what you are trying to accomplish (vision and strategy), and how you expect to accomplish those outcomes together (culture), clear and understood.

Think about it as if you're trying to create a menu that provides meal options for defined segments of your organization. First you might establish some common rules, such as asking that each of the segments include the main course and one or more of the three vegetables listed on your menu. But beyond that, it's up to them; let them decide if there will be an appetizer, a salad, extra sides, or a dessert.

In the real world, it might look like this: You ask the leaders of your key business units and central support functions to take the lead in designing performance solutions that best fit their teams' needs. You inform the design leads that all employees should complete quarterly goals in support of the company's articulated strategy (the main course). Your three vegetable options include a social media goal and feedback process, a project-based expectations and shared-planning template, and a monthly key metrics scorecard (targeted more to your manufacturing- or metrics-driven teams). The other add-on options (the appetizers and desserts) might include a mentoring program, planned talent review discussions, a peer recognition program, a role-based competency assessment tool that requires their support to build out, and team goal setting.

Create these menu items only after thinking about what your talent mix looks like and how that mix creates different needs across your employee groups. With the menu in place, you'll just play waiter or waitress, offering guidance but letting them make their own choices. Not only does this approach allow your teams to consider what works best for them but also I'm betting you'll find that the menu grows over time as your various teams create new methods and tools that work for their groups. If managed well, these ideas can be captured, shared, and adopted by others across the organization.

At this point, you are probably beginning to recognize that this approach turns the role played by traditional HR teams on its head. Today, HR typically designs and pushes standards, then spends months managing compliance with those standards. This shift lets the HR team have a lot more fun than they would merely policing policy, and it opens up the opportunity for them to create choices, tools, and content that focus on helping people improve their performance, connect to the company vision, and grow their careers.

Fundamental Shift #5: Welcome more voices to the conversation.
Shift from: A chosen few
Shift to: Diverse input and rich dialogue

If you really want a thought-provoking conversation at a dinner party, you don't invite just a few people who all have the same point of view on the same subjects. Or worse, just one person. You invite a variety of people with diverse backgrounds, points of view, and experience.

Similarly, you shouldn't rely on just one manager to provide feedback. Remember, we human beings are fallible and biased, and our scope of understanding and awareness is limited. This doesn't mean subjecting each employee to running a gauntlet of managers, though. Instead, build a culture in which employees receive ongoing, real-time feedback and training not only from managers, but from peers and colleagues as well.

Interestingly, Globoforce's 2013 survey on employee recognition found that 90 percent of their respondents said feedback from peers is more accurate than feedback provided just by an employee's supervisor or manager.[11] In addition to having the best perspective on one another's work, they often build relationships of trust and camaraderie that managers can't hope to emulate. They are in the perfect position to help one another grow and develop toward their individual goals. However, this happens in an organization only where it is safe to give and receive feedback and where people feel that they are part of a community, growing and learning together.

And how do you build this culture? you ask. Here are some areas to consider as you make this shift.

> *Stop talking about inclusion and engagement and start including and engaging in every conversation, every meeting.*
> —SUSAN SCOTT, FIERCE LEADERSHIP[12]

Start with your leaders

I've witnessed the direct connection between good leaders and healthy cultures time and time again. As Childress and Senn discuss in their book *The Secret of a Winning Culture:* "In most cases the corporate culture is a direct reflection of the senior team, a phenomenon called 'Shadow of the Leader.'"[13] Employees take their cues from their leaders, both collectively and individually. If your executive leaders are not open to feedback and are not willing to share their own successes and failures with honesty and humility, then building an open, growth-oriented culture is going to be a hard road, if not downright impossible. Try creating shared goals among the executive team that are made known across the organization, inviting leaders to company forums where they can share stories of their own lessons learned, and ensuring that leaders are seen both celebrating successes and acknowledging when things didn't go quite as expected in an open and transparent manner.

Recognize that your managers will make or break your attempt to create a culture of feedback

It is essential that you grow, hire, and reward managers who encourage open discussion and feedback. Effective managers don't punish people when they express ideas or concerns, and they will listen to all ideas and implement the best. They'll seek out their people frequently to understand how things are going, what's working, and what's not. They are willing and driven to provide feedback in the moment, and they stretch their teams to do their best work.

Your managers' readiness for this role cannot be taken for granted. Ask yourself if you even have the right managers. Were they selected for their ability to engage and lead teams, or were they selected for their technical competence? You'd be surprised how frequently the answer is the latter. Once you've confirmed that your organization has a strong set of managers, take the time to build their skills. Be clear on what you expect. Give them the tools they need, and let them know how they're doing. This is all beginning to sound rather familiar, yes?

Look at the processes and systems that influence everyday experiences

Take stock in your core business and people processes, and establish daily norms that encourage transparency and feedback. For example, make the communication of team and individual goals public. If your team captures lessons learned after projects or events, share those learnings with others in the organization who are likely to face similar challenges. Post client or customer feedback openly. Here's a simple example from my own team:

At PeopleFirm we ask each employee to create a yearly "postcard to the Tribe." The purpose and instructions are simple: "Outline your goals and commitments for the upcoming year." Employees consider what they want to achieve personally, how they will contribute to the organization's goals, and what they need from others to get there. Then they share this information with the entire company. That way, everyone knows what each of us is seeking to accomplish and contribute, and it helps us to understand how we can help each other and where feedback is most relevant. Many of this year's postcards are hanging on a wall in the office kitchen as I write, and all are shared virtually through our collaboration tools.

When building a culture that encourages greater feedback, never forget that a great place to start is with you and your own team. Ask for feedback on your own work, and accept it gracefully. Share your own goals and aspirations. Ask your team or peers for their help in reaching them. And make it clear to your team members that you expect them to do the same with one another.

Try crowdsourcing

Given the collaboration tools available to us today, crowdsourcing is an excellent way to add more voices to the mix. For example, you might poll all employees for input on outstanding individual performances throughout the year as a way to assign bonuses or performance awards. Or you might make formal or informal requests to the entire group for feedback on systems, customer trends, or investment decisions. And because crowdsourcing is most effective when implemented through a Web or social media platform, it's also an ideal way to reach those plugged-in millennials.

Consider talent reviews

If managed well, talent reviews can be another very effective means of adding more voices to the mix. A *talent review* is a conversation in which managers from cross-functional teams come together to share goals, accomplishments, and insights about their own teams while also seeking the input of others. A positive and open talent review conversation should provide greater visibility into the talent across the organization, create more understanding of key peer groups, increase each manager's understanding of how his or her team members are perceived, and help identify career opportunities for individuals that may cross team or functional boundaries. This will serve both to enhance a manager's perspective and to promote a culture of feedback.

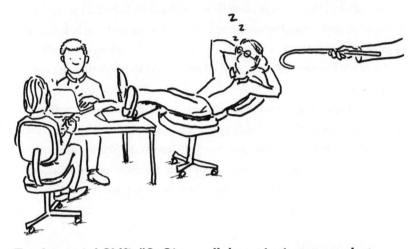

Fundamental Shift #6: Stop policing, start empowering.

Shift from: Control and oversight
Shift to: Managing by exception

I'm betting by now you get that one of my hobbyhorses is that control and oversight doesn't lead to better performance. It might make us feel better, more confident, and, well, in control. But all that oversight comes at a price, one that's paid by the individuals who engineer and operate our traditional structured performance programs, the organizations that invest in the process, and the employees, who bear the burden of the process. If we hadn't wasted so much on the controls, systems, templates, tracking mechanisms, rating debates, audits, and oversight, it would be almost comical that we've done all this work for questionable results. Maybe later we'll all have a good laugh when we look back at this period and shake our grizzled heads. Until then, we've got some work to do to bring down this beast that we've created.

This shift is about questioning the rigor we've built into our one-size-fits-all, manager-led models. It's about asking ourselves if the control and oversight is needed. On a deeper level, it comes down to having that heart-to-heart conversation with ourselves about why we thought we needed all that rigor to begin with. Often the need for control sits more with us than with our people, due to our inability to select qualified employees or our personal inability to let go. You hired these people because you felt they were the best candidates for the job, you've trained them to do their jobs well, and they've demonstrated that they're capable of doing what they were hired to achieve. But now can you bring yourself to back off and give them the space to do it their way? If so, that autonomy will lead to better work, stronger engagement, and improved odds of delivering on the company's goals.

Since autonomy won't get you to perfection, we still need a solution to deal with problem situations and difficult people when the need arises—and of course, it will. We all make hiring mistakes, and no matter how great a hiring manager you are, there will always be people who need additional attention. I can't deny that we deal with these issues in the normal course of leading teams of people, and I'm certainly not suggesting that you throw up your hands and ignore them when they arise. Quite the contrary. My advice is to address disruptive or inappropriate behavior, poor work, excessive absenteeism, heinous mistakes, or any other bad juju immediately. But here's the thing: we don't need an overengineered system that burdens all our employees with make-work documentation in order to be ready to take action in these individual situations.

The big idea is to manage these problem situations as the exceptions they are. Let's imagine that you have an employee who isn't performing well, and your newly designed approach to managing performance doesn't include a documented annual review. What do you do? Simple. Talk to him or her immediately. Discuss the issue and how it can be fixed. If you feel the situation warrants it, start your documentation as soon as you become aware that things are going off-track. This allows you to capture a simple, uncluttered account of what's happening, unencumbered by checklists, ratings, and competency assessments.

So perhaps it's time to switch the focus of some of our work-place policies and use them to unshackle the hardworking majority rather than inhibit the less noble minority. If you think people in your organization are predisposed to rip you off, maybe the solution isn't to build a tighter, more punitive set of rules. Maybe the answer is to hire new people.

—DANIEL H. PINK, *DRIVE: THE SURPRISING TRUTH ABOUT WHAT MOTIVATES US*[14]

It may surprise you to learn that this exception-based approach is quite likely to present less legal risk than what most of us are doing today. Corporate lawyers have told me that many of the annual reviews written today fail to call out these "off the tracks" performance issues, leaving organizations on poor legal footing. In fact, too often reviews look largely the same for average performers as they do for poor performers. Think about it: having no documentation at all would be preferable to documentation that makes the troubled employee look as if he or she is sailing along with no problems. I've yet to talk to any HR team that hasn't found itself caught between reality and what the review says. When performance has gone off the tracks, you can avoid this bind by creating one-off documentation in the moment, when the issue is fresh in your mind. That way, you're far more likely to have something that accurately reflects the situation. In addition to minimizing risk, this approach spares managers the burden of providing feedback for a troubled performer while their plate is already full with producing reviews for others.

You can see why I'm a proponent of managing by exception. Capture what needs to be captured, and take the burden of documentation off the broader team. Move quickly when action is needed, and keep things simple, factual, and direct.

The point of this fundamental shift is that one should address bad behavior when it happens—*but back off when things are going fine.* If it ain't broke, don't fix it. As managers, most of us struggle to keep control of our people and their performance, when we really should just let them do what they need to do and only step in when something arises that requires our attention (or if we're asked, of course).

If you're anything like me, you just read that last bit with a sense of relief. After all, simply trusting your employees is a lot easier than constantly stressing out about how to rein them in and stay on top of everything they're doing. You'll save yourself some headaches while seeing improved performance from people to boot. Autonomy for them, less stress and better results for you: it's truly a win-win.

Fundamental Shift #7: Incent collaboration.
Shift from: Individual metrics
Shift to: Shared commitments

What I love about collaboration is that it's both good for the organization (driving better products, ideas, and solutions) and good for your employees. It provides them with more opportunities to scale their ideas and to influence corporate actions, and it allows them to find greater meaning in their work because they can better appreciate the role they play in the broader corporate community.

> *If you want teamwork, you have got to recognize the team.*
>
> —EDWARD LAWLER,
> INFLUENTIAL MANAGEMENT THEORIST[15]

We've also come to realize that true, sustainable innovation requires collaboration. Today's most innovative companies don't have some Leonardo da Vinci sitting in a corner coming up with all the good ideas. Innovation comes from many things, but a key ingredient is a collaborative environment where ideas are shared, people can safely challenge the status quo and each other, and teams work together to explore and adopt new technologies, solutions, and ideas.

And then there's the fact that collaboration is itself a powerful motivator. Research shows that giving people team goals rather than just individual goals increases productivity and that it's even better if you make your individual and group goals compatible.[16] We evolved as a species to work together to support the common goal—so much so that our brain chemistry is designed to reward us for behavior that supports teamwork.[17] Think about that for a moment. Now think about how often we rate people on individual metrics. Basically, we've put systems in place to make people work in ways that are contrary to their own brain chemistry and in support of behaviors that we don't want to encourage, such as taking a "me" focus versus a "we" focus, or resorting to shortcuts to achieve target metrics, or getting to the goal come hell or high water, leaving a trail of tears behind them.

Despite what science and research have told us about motivation and teams, typical management practices continue to be primarily focused on the individual, stressing how each person is performing against defined expectations. Can you imagine how much more effective we could be if we tapped into the power of teamwork instead? To do so, try shifting the focus from individual performance metrics to a goal (or goals) the team can work toward together, such as a sales or delivery goal, or the customer service performance metrics of the team as a whole. As they share goals, team members will also share support, ideas, help when it's needed, and a laugh or two along the way—all ideal ingredients for engagement and productivity.

There's probably some part of you that's hesitant about moving away from managing at the individual level. It is a little counterintuitive in a culture that celebrates and rewards personal achievement. After all, you don't give an entire class a grade. But think about what would happen if you did! The class would work together to make sure that the work got done and would reach a higher level of performance as a whole. Your highest achievers might feel held back a little, or maybe they'll be energized by the influence they have on the team. But in an environment of collaboration, you will see the true leaders—your future managers—rise to the top as the group recognizes and celebrates those with outstanding contributions.

At this point, I often get asked about accountability. Yes, of course you need to have clear accountabilities, but those accountabilities for individuals are in reference to what the *team* is counting on them to deliver, not how they perform in isolation. It is a subtle shift from "Here's what I'm going to do this year" to "Here's how I will contribute to our group achievements," but it's an important one.

If you go down this road, you'll need to have certain elements in place to ensure success. First, get clear on what group of people you define as "the team." At PeopleFirm, we think of the entire company as the team, but for larger organizations that may not make as much sense. Second, be sure the endgame is clearly defined and known by everyone on the team you've identified. Be sure that everyone involved can articulate the outcome, destination, or result that the group as a whole is seeking. Third, create a safe environment for the team through mechanisms they can use to share feedback, talk about how things are working, escalate concerns, and periodically assess how they're doing as a unit. Fourth, be sure that each individual knows the part she's expected to play, and make sure that she has the capabilities she needs to deliver on that part. It's cruel for a team to expect something from someone who simply doesn't have the knowledge or ability to deliver on an expectation. Lastly, everyone in the group must be clear not only about his or her own role, but also about the roles and expectations of each contributor. It's like making a beautiful mosaic: the planned design needs to be understood, each person needs to be willing and able to provide his or her piece of the mosaic, the group needs to understand how all the pieces fit, and there needs to be clear intention in how the pieces come together.

Fundamental Shift #8: Get real with rewards.

Shift from: Paying for performance
Shift to: Paying for capabilities and rewarding for contributions

Linking pay to performance rarely works to drive sustained levels of performance. Instead, research continues to show us that people are much more motivated by *intrinsic* rewards, meaning that they work harder and better when they are doing things they find personally rewarding.[18] In the corporate world, this translates into things like enjoying the work itself, feeling like a valued part of the team, or being motivated by the company mission.

The rewards mantra for many years has been "pay for performance," yet when I work with clients who say this is their rewards strategy, I rarely see a strong connection between their pay incentives and differentiated performance. In practice, these "incentives" are often watered down to small merit increases with minimal variation between performance levels. So what gives?

I understand why this topic makes people nervous. It's complicated and personal. But maybe if we break it down, we can make it a little less scary. First, let's talk about pure base pay—the money we pay to our employees for the capabilities, knowledge, and work they provide. While we tend to overcomplicate it, the truth is that (just like when buying shoes or veggies) everything has a market value (in this case, talent), and we should pay market price for it. This is essentially what most of us are already looking at when we onboard new hires, whether we realize it or not. We do a salary survey and then base an employee's pay on what we're seeing in the market for similar skills and experience. The salary then increases as the employee gains expertise and participates in training, and therefore becomes more valuable to the employment market. Simple enough.

But too often we complicate it, adding in merit qualifications and adjusting the increases based on our assessment of performance. While we're doing this, we're either trying to keep within a market range or ignoring the market range entirely in the cases where the market has inconveniently moved beyond our allocated increase. We've all overheard one employee advise another, "You have to leave and return if you truly want to get back to market pay." And what happens if you pay too much for an employee who had a few great years but now is just coasting? Or if you have an employee who has decided to take a role below her market capability? Or if you have a hyperperformer that you can't recognize because of increase percentage constraints as a result of a poor economy or year? Our tendency to dole out small merit increases year after year limits our ability to deal with these situations. And in the end, we often come up with salary figures that have been influenced by such a large variety of factors that they've lost the purity of where we started in the first place.

It doesn't have to be like that. It's time to get real with rewards.

Consider linking pay to the market value of an employee's capability, experiences, and competencies and sticking with it. Ditch all the little incremental performance raises and other complicating factors. Keep it clean. When employees log new experiences, build new skills, and extend their capabilities, pay them more based on market value. If they don't log any, they don't get paid more. Of course, you need to keep your pay scale at market value, so that may mean incorporating cost-of-living increases into your approach. Tying pay to capabilities takes a little more faith than our traditional merit-increase model. Having a clear idea of what capabilities, skills, and experiences you value for each organizational role and what those elements are worth in the marketplace will allow you to make these compensation decisions with confidence.

But doesn't there have to be some financial reward for high performance?

Well, sure. But is a 2 percent pay raise based on your performance last year what really makes you put in that extra effort?

Instead, reward for goals that have been met or exceeded, especially group or company-wide performance goals. In other words, give bonuses instead of pay raises for outstanding contribution. Your team surpassed its production goals? The perfect opportunity for a shared bonus. An employee exceeded your expectations? Again, the ideal reason for a spot bonus. This way, you're motivating your employees to continue to learn and develop throughout their careers in order to increase their base salary, while motivating them to excel and work as a team in order to achieve the on/off bonuses. I like to sum all this up with the phrase "pay for capability, reward for contribution™."

So far, all I've talked about here is money-based rewards, and if I've said it once, I've said it a million times: money is not the best motivator. Here are a few alternatives:

- Manager or supervisor praise (obvious, but so often overlooked)
- Formal or informal peer-based rewards programs
- Time with leaders, gurus, and recognized influencers within an organization
- Exciting new project assignments and opportunities and time in the spotlight
- Training or other learning opportunities
- Time off
- Thank-you cards (your mother told you to write them, remember?)
- Awards and other forms of customized recognition

When considering noncash rewards, it's important to remember that recognition doesn't have to be limited to management. In fact, peer-based models can have an immensely positive influence on creating a culture of collaboration and transparency. Most individuals value recognition from their peers, whether shared on a one-to-one basis or celebrated with the team. As I mentioned in Fundamental Shift #5, it is valuable and healthy to include more people in the conversation, and that holds true for both feedback and recognition. After all, recognition is simply another form of positive feedback. So don't just think top-down; consider engaging your whole team in the recognition process.

This is one place where being small is an advantage, because when you're small, you don't need to make this complicated. At PeopleFirm, we've been able to do this in a low-overhead kind of way by simply giving our Tribe what we call PeopleFirm Buck$. In a typical year, we distribute about $500 in cash to each Tribe member. We entrust this money to our employees and send them off with a mission: to use it to recognize their peers. In return, we ask that they track what they spend, share their recognition with us, and spend their money wisely. It's been a smashing success. It's created a stronger culture of recognition, and the personalization and care that have gone into some of the gifts have truly blown me away. One of my favorite examples is that of a team that pitched in to buy their project manager a plane ticket to visit her son who had recently started college in the Midwest. They knew how much she was missing him. Do you think she'll easily forget that personalized recognition—that reward for her contributions? Not a chance.

New Thought, Thoughtfully Applied

Now that we've taken a hard look at many of the existing assumptions that have dogged traditional performance management and explored ways to shift away from those ideas and toward better solutions, it's time to define exactly what we're trying to accomplish with all this effort—the final piece of the puzzle before we move on to designing your new approach to performance management.

Chapter 4

THE THREE COMMON GOALS

BEFORE WE HIT THAT REBOOT BUTTON, let's get absolutely clear on what performance management is and why we do it.

Because of its management-by-objectives roots, traditional performance management has historically operated as an individual's scorecard of accomplishments (or failings). However, in recent years we've seen more organizations try to do more with their performance management programs, using them as a means to focus on the development of the individual employee and to link individual goals to company objectives. HR professionals talk about a variety of goals they hope to achieve, including "differentiated distribution of rewards, based on individual performance";[1] "creating a high performance culture"; "ensuring equitable compensation";[2] or "providing employee coaching and mentoring."

As varied (and jargon laden) as those responses are, they are all perfectly valid answers. Each organization is unique, with different levels of maturity, mixtures of employee demographics, and diverse cultures and values that have evolved over time. That uniqueness means they tend to weigh some outcomes more heavily than others; one team, for instance, might place a higher priority on aligning strategies, another on developing talent. Yet, despite these variances, most organizations are trying to meet their desired outcomes by doing the same thing as everyone else. Doesn't it seem a little crazy that we're investing so much time and resources trying to create experiences that are unique to our organization's wants and needs, yet we're so often still grabbing that dusty off-the-shelf performance management manual published in 1950 in hopes that it will get us there? No matter how many bells and whistles we might add, they can't disguise the fact that the solutions we're arriving at just aren't cutting it.

So when getting clear on the goals of performance programs, we begin by accepting that each organization's expectations will not be exactly the same. However, to understand these differences, it is helpful to anchor our thinking with a basic framework. This framework defines what I call the Three Common Goals. It represents the universal outcomes of strong performance programs, desired outcomes that have become clear to me in my research and my quarter-century of consulting. Think of these three interrelated goals as the essence of all performance programs and the basis from which each organization's unique differences evolve. More simply, consider them the fundamental building blocks for the design project ahead of us.

Performance Management's Three Common Goals

In my experience, every organization is ultimately using its performance management program to develop its people's skills and capabilities, reward all of its employees equitably, and drive overall organizational performance by ensuring that team and individual goals are aligned and reflect the goals of the organization. In other words, I believe that the Three Common Goals of any performance program should be as shown in figure 4.1:

Figure 4.1 The Three Common Goals of Performance Management

1	*Develop People*	• *Individual development* • *Coaching and mentoring* • *Retention of top performers* • *Leadership development* • *Succession planning*
2	*Reward Equitably*	• *Pay for contribution* • *Promotion and advancement* • *Total rewards*
3	*Drive Organizational Performance*	• *Goal alignment* • *Strategic communications* • *Culture development*

How these goals are prioritized or emphasized—what "good" looks like related to each goal—will differ from organization to organization. So, too, will the way in which each organization sets about making those goals a reality. But any high-performing organization will have some combination of these three ingredients in its performance management recipe.

In the next chapter, we'll explore how you can design your own modern approach to performance, anchored by these three goals. But first, let's get familiar with our ingredients.

Goal #1: Develop people

It seems obvious that the development of employees should be a key outcome of any performance solution. After all, isn't that what performance reviews and career discussions are all about? Well, yes, they should be. But as we discussed earlier, this objective is often the one that loses out. And things get especially muddled when we get hung up on our rewards and ratings processes. As they say, the road to hell is paved with good intentions.

So let's think about what a strong performance management solution truly focused on developing people might look like. First, it would provide in-the-moment coaching, helping individuals to understand what went well and what could be enhanced the next time around. We all know this intuitively, but many of us are so used to stockpiling this feedback for the annual review that we don't do this for our employees. Further, they'd receive suggestions to support their growth in an environment that would allow them to absorb the suggestions without feeling threatened or having something at risk (like their pay raise).

Next, individuals would also have information at their disposal that would provide insight into what is expected in their current role and any future roles to which they hope to advance. Resources for development might include mentors or coaches who are their advocates within the organization. There also could be self-assessment and training tools that would link to their development plan, providing ideas and resources to support their unique goals.

Admittedly, I've just given you a very employee-centric view of the *develop people* goal. But let's not forget the value that this goal, when well-executed, brings to our organizations as a whole. For one thing, offering a performance program with a strong emphasis on developing people gives employers a rich view of their inventory of talent. Those employee assessment tools and other resources benefit the organization as well as employees by providing insight into the skills our people have, what capabilities we might easily grow, and what skills and capabilities are missing or at risk. What's more, they can tell us how individuals want to advance their careers and how well their personal goals align to the direction of the organization. And don't forget that if the program engages and empowers employees to take greater ownership and gives them a sense of involvement in their career decisions—which it would—then we'll see employee engagement and retention increase.

Need proof? A 2010 Executive Conference Board study showed a direct correlation between employee satisfaction/engagement and the degree of employee involvement in job design decisions. They noted that being aligned with their job interest is the single most important driver of commitment for employees.[3] And while we don't have the data to tie performance programs directly to increased organizational performance, the linkage between employee engagement and organizational performance is well supported by years of research.[4, 5, 6]

So, how well does your current program deliver enhanced people development? I'm betting the answer is "Not so well." And that's understandable—more often than not, HR leaders and management are too preoccupied with overseeing and managing their annual performance processes to focus on developing their people or on providing the tools to empower individuals to own their development. It's high time we changed how we spend our time.

Goal #2: Reward equitably

This is the ingredient that I find most often confounds people when they are looking at building a new performance solution. It's the dimension that most often gets in the way of doing something different from what we have always done. So let's take a little time to be sure that we understand it and the role it plays in performance programs.

First, let's be clear on what the words really mean. Equitable is defined by the Oxford Dictionary as "fair and impartial." It's important to note that equally and equitably are not the same thing. For example, let's say you worked for three weeks writing a strategy for a new business unit, and your peer proofread it and tuned it up for you over the past few days. I'd sure hope you'd want your peer to receive some recognition for her support, but I doubt you'd be happy if her reward and recognition was equal to yours. Instead, you'd want the recognition to be equitable, meaning that each of you would get as much credit as you deserved.

When organizations speak of differentiated pay and rewards, then, they are looking for those rewards to be distributed in an equitable manner—fairly, unbiased, and consistent with the level of contribution or impact. It's also important to note that rewarding equitably is not just about pay. We're talking about total rewards: compensation, formal and informal recognition, benefits, promotions, project assignments, you name it.

From an employee's perspective, equity is all about fairness. It's natural for employees to ask themselves questions like "Am I fairly paid for my skills?" "Am I recognized and rewarded fairly compared with those around me?" "Are reward decisions being made in a fair and unbiased manner?" Remember Fatal Flaw #8: We are not Pavlov's dog? While extrinsic rewards are rarely a driver of human behavior, the belief that a system is unfair or biased is a significant driver in dissatisfaction. In other words, confidence that the system is equitable makes for happy and engaged employees.

However, only about a third of employees feel that their current performance management programs are resulting in equitable rewards.[7] Even worse, according to the Corporate Executive Board's 2013 study Breakthrough Performance in the New Work Environment, fewer than one in four HR executives (the leaders who seemingly should support it) believe that their current performance management system reflects true employee performance.[8]

In my discussions with HR and business leaders, two concerns relating to equitable rewards surface again and again. The first is that while most organizations intend to deliver differentiated rewards and often have publicly made a commitment to do so, the slight variations between a top performer and a moderate performer are seldom likely to pass a test of true differentiation (except in the cases of highly measurable areas like sales). Too often, the budgeted and allocated compensation ranges are so narrow that it's nearly impossible to deliver on the intent to provide differentiated rewards across employee performance levels. In other words, trying to recognize star performers for their contributions and differentiate their increase from your solidly second-tier performers when you have a budgeted increase range of only 4 or 5 percent is pretty much impossible. For many managers, this exercise is frustrating at best, and at worst it reinforces the view that they're as much pawns in the game of performance management as those they're reviewing.

The second concern that HR/talent leaders frequently share with me is that they're stuck on how to distribute rewards equitably without a numbers-driven rating system that comes with strong oversight and control from the compensation team. Without alignment, support, and collaboration between the functional teams that own the performance process and the compensation or total rewards plan, they are stuck. I get it. We need to recognize that many compensation teams have made a science out of their compensation models. They've spent years doing the research, building the models, and getting the executives and board to buy in. To walk away from that investment in order to trade it in for a people-powered process is not an easy shift to make.

But something has to give, or we'll just keep treading water. First, you need to get a clear view of what reward equitably means to your organization and how you can best achieve that goal in your unique environment. Second, you'll need to ensure that you build a shared understanding of your vision and secure the early support of key stakeholders, like the people who own the total rewards process, before you ever get started. And then, of course, I recommend putting in place a "pay for capability, reward for contribution" program as outlined in Fundamental Shift #8. Base your pay on the market value of your employees' skills and experience; then grant bonuses for exceptional work. Simple as that.

Goal #3: Drive organizational performance

The goal of driving organizational performance is probably the most recent addition to our collective thinking on performance management. This is not surprising, given the increasing amount of research that has demonstrated the correlation between an employee's connectedness to the mission and vision of his or her company and the measurable performance of that organization. The alignment of employees with strategy and business goals is a hallmark of high-performing organizations; in fact, high-performing organizations are two and a half times more likely than lower performing organizations to get this key to successful execution right.[9]

Gallup further validates this finding in its Q12 employee engagement survey, which asks respondents to indicate agreement with the following statement: "The mission or purpose of my company makes me feel my job is important." Its extensive research shows that there is a direct correlation between how employees rate that one question and employee retention, customer metrics, productivity, and profitability. Gallup concludes that "the best workplaces give their employees a sense of purpose, help them feel they belong, and enable them to make a difference."[10] Simply stated, we now understand how important it is to ensure that teams and individuals are fully aligned to the goals of the company.

On a human level, I'm talking about individuals and teams feeling an emotional connection to the purpose of the organization. That means they understand the vision, they believe in it, they want to be a part of it, and they see how their work and roles contribute to the broader goal. While I strongly believe that connecting emotionally is where you get the biggest bang for your buck, that connection also must translate into a framework that helps each employee make good decisions and focus on the right work, day in and day out. Most current talent management systems have solved for this by including functionality in their performance management modules that enables cascading goals. This technical execution of goal alignment enables the cascade of an organization's strategic goals to teams and managers, in some cases going so far as to distribute managers' goals across their teams on a weighted basis. For example, if my goal as an IT manager is to deliver a new application at the end of the quarter, then I might distribute the work across my team, allocating the more complicated coding to the more experienced and proven development resources, while ensuring that each team member has been assigned a piece of the total application.

Drive organizational performance might sound as if it has more to do with the organization than the employee, but it doesn't. Sure, organizations want their teams and employees aligned, doing the right work, and not wasting time on efforts that are off-strategy. But we have to recognize that, as humans, we also crave the feeling of being a part of something. Most people want to feel that the work they are doing is important and purposeful. This connectedness is a vital part of an employee's career satisfaction and overall performance, and considering its value to both the organization and the individual, we have to find ways to make sure that it happens.

Let's Abandon the Knotted Solution

One of the most notable challenges posed by our traditional approach to performance management is that we've tried to deliver all three of these goals in one highly integrated solution that is often overly complex and poorly defined. We rarely start with a clear view of the importance of each goal to our organization, or the implications that each goal presents to our team. In other words, we're building from the top down rather than from the bottom up. What's more, we are often fuzzy on how interconnected each of these goals should be within the design of our solution. For example, can we answer questions like "Does the effort that individuals invest in their own development affect how they will be rewarded?" or "Are individuals' contributions to the articulated goals of the organization the only things that influence their rewards?" Very few of us can. This lack of clarity regarding the three goals of performance management and how they relate to one another is, I believe, a significant reason why so many organizations have no idea where to start in creating a better solution.

If an organization doesn't do the work to assess the Three Common Goals and answer the hard questions in the context of its own unique culture, it isn't going to get very far toward a new solution.

I find that when an important concept needs to be well anchored (and understanding the Three Common Goals is an important concept), it helps to have a visual image. When working with clients, we like to use the simple analogy of a bicycle frame as that visual support. So ride along with me for a minute as I explain this visual aid.

Selecting the Right Frame

A bike frame—though essentially a triangle—can vary based on the purpose, style, size, and expected usage of the bike. One side may be longer than another, the thickness of the frame may change, and all three points of the core frame may or may not be connected. A bike's frame may have a small or large triangle at the core, depending on the rider and the bike's purpose.

Figure 4.2 The Three Common Goals visualized on a "performance management bike."

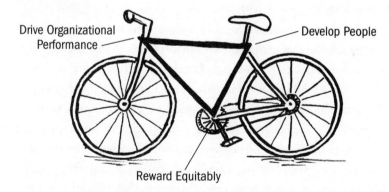

Drive Organizational Performance

Develop People

Reward Equitably

Now apply that concept to the frame of your performance management bike, which is made up of the Three Common Goals: *develop people, drive organizational performance,* and *reward equitably* (see figure 4.2). While all three goals are likely to be present in your performance management bike, how pronounced each goal is and how connected the three are to each other should vary from organization to organization. If you're a mature global consumer products company, your performance management bike is likely to look different from the one that the forty-person design firm down the street just built, just as a Tour de France racing model will differ from your child's first push bike.

Riding the Wrong Bike

The problem with performance management today is that we've all been riding pretty much the same performance management bike for far too long, and more often than not we keep pulling that same model out of storage every year without much thought about whether it has the unique features we need to drive real performance in today's world. In earlier chapters we explored how the world has changed, touched on many of the advances in our insight on motivation and collaboration, and exposed traditional PM's shortcomings in meeting these changes.

With that knowledge as our foundation, we now recognize that, metaphorically speaking, we're simply not going to see a true competitor pulling up to the starting line of the Tour de France with a banana-seat bike decked out with training wheels, a daisy basket, and streamers. When elite performance is required, this kind of bike is a joke—as is the idea that conventional performance management will get today's organizations, including yours, where they want to go.

Part II

REDESIGN.

In matters of style, swim with the current; in matters of principle, stand like a rock.

—Thomas Jefferson

I'M A FIRM BELIEVER IN PROCESS, especially when it comes to designing performance solutions. When you begin a project of this nature, it's important to follow an established design and implementation progression. A clearly defined process means you'll be making the right moves in the right order, and you'll also be able to keep the people you're bringing with you on this journey in the loop. In other words, a strong process anchors your design team, keeps everyone on the same page, and helps the team know what's expected, when it's expected, and what's coming next.

For all those reasons (and more), I've defined a simple five-phase process for us to follow. For each phase I provide the supporting steps and corresponding tools and techniques that I hope will allow you to design and implement your unique solution thoughtfully while still maintaining forward momentum. In a nutshell, the PM Reboot process looks like this:

Mobilize	*Sketch*	*Configure*	*Build*	*Implement*
Plan, invite participants, and get started	Align on your principles of design	Configure, test, and validate your solution	Build your solution, manage dependencies	Plan the change, implement, and evaluate

The PM Reboot process

In this section, Redesign, we will cover the first three phases—one chapter each for Mobilize, Sketch, and Configure. We'll wrap up by bringing the work of these three phases to life with real-world examples. Later, in Part III, Reboot, we'll explore the final two phases of this process (Build and Implement), and take a look at the important topic of building buy-in and ensuring the adoption of your newly minted and designed solution. I should warn you that in both parts 2 and 3 I'm going to get a little geeky with you (let's chalk it up to the engineer in me coming out). My mission is to walk you through a design process that will help translate the Fundamental Shifts into a carefully considered, ready-to-implement, and greatly improved performance management solution, and there's no way to do that without getting a bit technical in places. Fret not, though, because both of these sections are supported by a comprehensive **Toolbox,** where many of the tools and templates are shared in detail.

One last note before we get started with the PM Reboot process: in the end, you may find that you've built something you may not want to call "performance management." Depending on the choices you make to *drive organizational performance, develop people,* and *reward equitably,* your solution may not look anything like traditional performance management. In fact, I've banned the phrase at PeopleFirm. OK, maybe not actually banned, since that would go against our culture—but I am known for making a face whenever people use the term to describe our approach to the thing we call "Building Your Career." This kind of rebranding can be a very good thing, especially if the process you're using today is wildly unpopular with your team. There's nothing wrong with an image makeover along with your redesign, so ask your team for their ideas on what name best describes your new solution.

Chapter 5
MOBILIZE

Mobilize	*Sketch*	*Configure*	*Build*	*Implement*
Plan, invite participants, and get started	Align on your principles of design	Configure, test, and validate your solution	Build your solution, manage dependencies	Plan the change, implement, and evaluate

OUR FIRST STEP IS ALL ABOUT GETTING OURSELVES ORGANIZED AND READY. The success of any journey depends on building a plan and inviting the right people along, especially when you want to be sure that you have the support of those who are funding the trip. And that's where we're going to begin: by ensuring that our leaders are with us, building our plan, and inviting the other travelers we want to accompany us on the adventure.

Lead the Leaders

Let me tell you a memorable story that a client shared with me. As the chief human resources officer (CHRO), she had tasked her team with creating a vision piece about a new approach to performance to present to the executives. Her team excitedly built their recommendations. Bear in mind that this was high level; they were simply trying to gain support in order to move ahead with designing a new approach. The team came to the executive meeting inspired by their ideas and ready to roll. The speaker for the group, the CHRO's second-in-command, walked the executives through their proposal. The CHRO was thrilled; it was an excellent piece of work, and she was proud of her team and their creative boldness. As the presentation wrapped up, she started clapping with enthusiasm. None of the other executives joined in. In the awkward silence, the CEO turned to her and asked, "Why are you clapping?" And with that, their dreams to rethink their performance management program died, at least for the near term. Despite all the great prep work, they hadn't correctly calculated where the CEO and the executives were in their views, knowledge, and insight on this topic, and those leaders obviously weren't ready to hear the team's proposal. This kind of disconnect is not uncommon, so I recommend that you get your arms around it sooner rather than later.

Let's face it: executive leaders often need special handling. Year after year, "lack of executive sponsorship" has been cited as the top reason for the failure of change programs.[1] And when it comes to performance strategies, I've found that a lack of executive support is often the thing that holds people back the most. More than anything else, it's why people *talk* about changing their approach but never seem to be able to really do it.

Executives don't resist these ideas because they are closed-minded people. Sure, some may be a little old-fashioned, but most still care about their teams, right? I think the main reason why executives frequently get left behind is that no one is willing to educate them, either because people feel that executives should already know this stuff due to the exalted role they play in the organization or because it's just too intimidating to sit down and talk openly about the drawbacks of the established ways of doing things. Sitting across the table, looking an executive in the eye, and telling him that everything he believes is wrong might very well feel like a potentially career-limiting move, no matter how much research you have to back you up. And so nobody does it, which means it's highly unlikely that executives are well versed in the subject of performance management—and even more unlikely that they know nearly as much about this subject as you do. This is where a little courage comes in.

Here's my thinking on this front: First, I encourage you to check your fear at the door and get comfortable with challenging this group— diplomatically, of course. I find that folks can let the intimidation factor play too large a role, sometimes to the point where they chicken out of the really tough conversations. Always keep in mind that you're coming to them with the intent of creating a healthier, happier organization. How can that be bad?

Here are a few tips on the special care and handling of leaders:

- *Get them thinking.* Don't just *tell* them; help them find their own way to the knowledge. Try starting off by asking who their best managers were earlier in their careers and what it was that made them great. Ask them about their own best and worst experiences with giving and receiving feedback, or with performance management in general. Make it personal. Capture what they share so that you can use their own words later as part of their education process. Help them imagine how a change could benefit the company and your people in powerful ways.

- *Educate them.* I find this to be the biggest miss when it comes to making your case to leadership. All too often, people assume that leaders know it all. Surely they don't, and how could they? Leaders simply don't have the time to seek out the information needed to make informed decisions on all aspects of the business. That's why they have experts like you. Your job is to take the time to educate them on this subject. You don't need to be condescending, of course, but do be explicit about helping them learn. Ask them to read part 1 of this book to get a better understanding of the Fatal Flaws, Fundamental Shifts, and Common Goals. If nothing else, it will give you a great place to start a conversation. Additionally, find similar organizations that have already made notable changes to their performance management programs, and see if you can coordinate a visit or a call to their CEOs to share ideas and successes. There's nothing like hearing about it from a peer. And, as you collect insights throughout the process, share them with your leaders.

- *Shift their focus to the future.* Engage your leaders in conversation about the future. Ask them to talk about the organization's strategy, and have them describe where the organization is heading. Take it a step further and talk with them about their legacy. What do they want to leave behind? What do they want to be their mark? Ask them to consider how these new performance solutions will help them to achieve those goals both operationally and personally.

All this sets the stage for asking that all-important question: "Are you with me?" If you do it right, your leaders will be. And you won't be the only one clapping.

Plan Your Journey

Borrowing the wise words of Stephen R. Covey (of *The 7 Habits of Highly Effective People* fame), let's "begin with the end in mind" and take a look at when it will make the most sense for your team to reboot your performance management.[2] Why is the *when* important? Because it's important to consider the rhythm of your business and how that rhythm implies (or in some cases imposes) a certain window of time or even a specific date for switching over to your new approach. For example, do you wrap up your traditional annual reviews at the end of the calendar year and set goals at the beginning of the new year? If so, then you should think about switching over to your new solution on January 1 of the coming year. That means having your design and build completed by the end of the third quarter of the prior year in order to have a quarter to unveil the new direction, signal the end of the old, and get your teams ready to use new tools and methods.

A number of other factors could dictate your schedule: everything from a new leader coming onboard to a new system in the offing or the acquisition of a new company. I find technology events, like the sunsetting of the old system that housed the performance management, to be the most common of these triggers. It's important to tune in to these technology-driven timelines because the last thing you want is to put your team through two related changes by implementing a new system and then having to do it again once you've finalized your process. Sadly, this cart-before-the-horse timing with system implementations happens all too often when IT and HR teams plan their projects separately. Whatever factors influence your timeline, the key at this stage is to get very clear on the planned implementation date and work backward from there to define a realistic journey plan. And by "realistic" I mean an achievable plan that allows you enough time to work through every phase of the project.

At this point, create the initial plan for how you expect your solution to roll out across your organization—how it will be staged, if you will. If you're a fairly compact group located mostly in one place, or the makeup of your employee segments is similar, then a "Big Bang" approach— bringing everybody with you in one fell swoop—may make the most sense. However, if your organization is more complex, you may want to start with a smaller, targeted team. In this case, pick one that's easily accessible or friendly to your cause.

For instance, I worked with a company that decided to reboot its retail stores first, designing and implementing a complete solution specifically for that audience. The leadership made the decision to start with the stores because they knew that the stores team was the place where they could have the greatest impact and deliver the most value. After the successful transition in the stores, they stepped back and began considering a solution for headquarters. While this allowed them to keep key features consistent across teams, it also empowered them to focus on the unique needs of the corporate culture and staff (as in Fundamental Shift #4—Abandon uniformity). After headquarters, they moved on to the warehouses. This staggered strategy allowed them not only to design for each specific group but also to get smarter as they went along so that they were able to build off the learnings from each preceding rollout.

I'm also a big fan of pilots. Pick a test group and engage them in a process that helps you to refine your solution and your messaging about it. Piloting your approach can be a great way to reduce adoption risk and prepare you for a much bigger implementation scope. Pilots have the added benefit of creating a group of highly engaged individuals who feel more connected to your new solution and can help build excitement and bring others along when you're ready.

My last word on this topic is that you should never hesitate to revise the plan. One of the greatest frustrations in my work is to watch teams get well into a project and learn things that change their core assumptions or timelines, and then turn a blind eye to this new information so they don't have to admit that the plan might need to be reassessed. Moving ahead with a poor plan is always a losing strategy, and I've seen it too many times in my career. Refine the plan along the journey. Periodically consider whether your assumptions have changed, if you're experiencing more resistance than planned, if you've discovered dependencies that are at risk, or even whether or not you can honestly make the timing work given the resources you have allocated. A good, realistic journey plan is a valuable asset, so take the time to carefully think it through—then let it evolve as needed.

SUPPORT AND BUY-IN CHECKPOINT

Throughout the process, I will offer these quick reminders on checking in with the executive sponsors, influential leaders, and others you've identified as important to keep close and tuned in. Managing change and ensuring adoption truly starts on day one. Taking these simple steps helps you to validate your thinking (therefore improving your outcomes), while also allowing you to gauge the nature of the support or resistance you can expect as you move toward implementation.

At this early point in the process, you want to be sure that you have agreement on the journey plan and timeline. Not only do you want the sponsors to be aligned with the plan, but also you need to consider other teams or individuals who have a stake in the timing of events. Perhaps the compensation team? Or the CIO? Maybe the people who drive your strategic–planning process? Or other groups within your talent management function, such as the workforce or succession planning team? Seek their input and give them a heads-up on those changes you know are coming—in short, bring them along with you on the journey.

Invite the Right People to the Conversation

Don't try this alone. If you want to take a group of people in a new direction, especially a direction that is different from the one they have always known, then you need to be sure that you bring the right people with you from the very beginning.

Here's the thing: Designing a new approach to performance takes good thinking. It demands tough decisions. And even once all the big thinking is done, you still have to do the work of building out the nuts and bolts of the solution. It's totally doable, of course. But what isn't very doable is designing a solution alone in a vacuum or with a small group of like-minded people and then expecting to bring the larger group happily along with you after the fact. For one thing, if you take that approach, your design process will likely lack the varying points of view that might take you in new and more interesting directions. For another, you're going to need champions of the change on your side to drive support and adoption when you're ready to unleash your beautiful new performance management solution on the team. If you want them with you when you're ready to say "Go," then you need them with you from the beginning. Engage them early and often.

Start by asking yourself these two questions:

1. Who should be part of my *design team?*

2. Who should be invited to the *conversation?*

You might wonder what the difference is between the "design team" and those merely "invited to the conversation." This is an important distinction. The design team is the group of people who will work with you, side by side, through the entire design process. The conversation invitees are those folks you will need with you metaphorically (that is, they're looped in and have your back) but who won't be involved in the day-to-day work.

Whom should you pick for your design team? Frequently, I see organizations selecting a mix of executives and HR leaders. The conversation needs to include executives, since it's vital that they be onboard; and obviously HR needs to play a key role in the design effort. But I prefer to see teams that go beyond those two groups in order to represent the diversity of the organization. That means inviting people from different employee segments, disciplines, functions, and locations. Include team members and other people leaders who will have a strong stake in the dialogue. I'm not telling you to build a huge design team; that comes with its own problems. I'm saying you should be creative about whom you invite. See how many boxes you can tick off with each individual.

In other words, the design team should be a small(ish) but diverse group that comes as close as you can to representing a cross-section of your organization. Of course, you want people on that team who are excited to take a fresh look at performance management. But it also never hurts to throw in a few doubters to help keep you on your toes; if all goes well, they may become your strongest advocates when all is said and done.

Figure 5.1 shows a simple example that looks a lot like a team we pulled together for one of my clients. In this case, we created a design group that nicely represented their global footprint as well as their mix of employee segments—and without inviting the entire company to the discussion.

Figure 5.1. Design team example.

	BUSINESS UNIT	FUNCTION	LOCATION	PEOPLE MANAGER	TENURE (YEARS)	SALARY/ HOURLY	UNION	HIGH PERFORMER
Fred	Rocks	Engineering	North America	Y	20+	S	Y	Y
Wilma	Dinosaurs	Design	HQ	Y	3-5	S	N	N
Betty	Kitchen	Production	Emerging Markets	N	5-10	H	Y	N
Barney	Bowling	HR	South America	Y	10-20	S	N	N
Pebbles	Toys	Supply Chain/HR	Singapore	N	1-3	H	N	Y
Bamm-Bamm	Clubs	Sales	Europe	N	<1	S	N	N
Dino	Corporate	Finance	HQ	Y	5-10	S	N	Y

Once our design team has been established, it's time to choose the larger and wider group of people we want to invite to the conversation. For some organizations, the conversation group may include the entire organization. For others, it may be only a select set of individuals. If you're picking a select set, then seek out those individuals who need to feel included, those who have expressed a desire to have a voice in your process, and those whose voices you want to be sure to include (such as big fans of your plan or people who could stop the whole effort in its tracks if they aren't with you).

A great way to get the selection process started is to ask your design team and invited-to-the-conversation leaders whom they think should be included. This broader conversation group should also include people whose voices are missing from your design team, perhaps certain constituencies or demographic groups whose views will make for a better end result. I'm thinking anyone from union representatives to the distribution team in Puerto Rico. Seek out differences in opinion, and make sure you have solid representation from your workforce.

This group requires special attention, and you'll hear me speak of them throughout the process. It is critical that they be engaged from the very beginning, which I recognize can be tough with such a diverse group. Here are a few methods you might use to engage your conversation group throughout your process, from seeking input on what's currently working (and what isn't) to validating your solution and rollout plans, and onward down the line:

- Lead focus group discussions.
- Task leaders to engage their teams and facilitate leadership-driven conversations.
- Crowdsource your questions.
- Design and deploy a simple survey.

One huge benefit of technology is that it gives us the ability to invite as many people as we want to the conversation. A great example of this is the process Adobe went through in designing its new performance management approach. The Adobe leaders were committed to cocreating the new solution alongside their employees. Their process included a very intentional crowdsourcing element in which they first notified employees of the plan to ditch stack ranking via a companywide blog post and then asked them to suggest what they wanted to do instead. They asked what needed to go, what should remain, and what employees thought should be added. Their approach yielded great results, and the leaders said that the crowdsourcing process crystallized their vision for the new approach.[3]

The headline here is that it's imperative that you engage your executives and key decision makers, as well as diverse voices in your company, in a process that includes reasoned discussion. Pose thoughtful questions that help them challenge the old thinking, expose flawed assumptions, and introduce new ideas. And throughout that conversation, shine a light on the factors driving your choices, introducing and building support for new ideas and approaches (like the Fundamental Shifts, for example) to gain alignment on the direction to which you are committed.

SUPPORT AND BUY-IN CHECKPOINT

Once your design team is selected and confirmed, be sure to loop back in with the leaders—both those who offered ideas for whom should be included and the managers who have direct reports who are participating in the design process. It is important that your executive sponsors know who's on the team and that they support your choices. It's also helpful to thank the managers of your design team members for letting their people participate. Also, remind them every once in a while of the important role their people are playing and the value they are creating for the organization. In fact, this is a great way to demonstrate your philosophy of recognition.

Chapter 6
SKETCH

Mobilize	*Sketch*	*Configure*	*Build*	*Implement*
Plan, invite participants, and get started	**Align on your principles of design**	Configure, test, and validate your solution	Build your solution, manage dependencies	Plan the change, implement, and evaluate

LEADERS ON BOARD? CHECK. JOURNEY PLAN? CHECK. DESIGN TEAM ENGAGED? CHECK. Now that we've *mobilized* for action, it is time to move to the Sketch phase of your journey. In this phase, your team will make choices about what is most important to include in your new performance management solution. Yes, it is time to start making some vital design decisions. And where does any good design begin? I think it starts with clarity on your starting place and alignment on your destination. Once there is alignment on the *from* and the *to,* then a good design needs a simple sketch that helps us visualize that destination. This sketch will be influenced by prioritized design principles and agreement on how to deliver any defined goals—in our case, the Three Common Goals of performance management.

Know Your Starting Place

Before you dive in, step back and take the time to make sure your design team is grounded in a common understanding of the facts about performance management. If you've done a good job of selecting a diverse team, it's unlikely that they are all going to be on the same page at this point—and that's OK. It's your job to get them there. You do this by arming them with a solid foundation, including the research I've shared about motivating people and building high-performing teams, and the role that performance management can play in driving those outcomes, both positively and negatively. Think back to the Fatal Flaws and the Fundamental Shifts. Knowledge is a wonderful gift, so share it. It is vital to have a common grounding in the failings of traditional performance management, as well as the potential of a new solution, before your team moves forward.

Next, I recommend that you spend time as a team understanding the current state of your organization. Figure 6.1 shows some possible items to look at:

Figure 6.1. Assessing the current state of your performance management.

PM Inventory	■ What does performance management look like in the company today? ■ Capture the current performance improvement process and timeline. What are all the steps involved? ■ Who owns the process, both the oversight and the steps within the process? ■ Collect examples of the tools and templates. ■ Have any teams or groups come up with their own alternative version or overall approach that works better for them?
Usage	■ What is the current level of usage—the real rate of adoption? ■ Does usage differ by team, geography, or some other variable? ■ How involved is HR or others in completing the process?
Perception	■ What's working? ■ What's not working? ■ Do managers and employees perceive it differently? ■ What's HR's assessment? ■ How engaged are your leaders in the process? Are they champions, are they indifferent, or do they hate it?

Employee Insights	▪ Gather your talent inventory data: number of employees, employee types, locations, levels, job families or functions, etc.
	▪ Do all employees engage with the performance improvement process in the same manner? If not, what are the differences?
	▪ Are features, tools, and sources available to all employees (e.g., mentoring or bonus programs)?
	▪ Are there events that occur only for select employee groups (e.g., talent reviews for VPs and above)?
Process Data	▪ How many reviews are completed each year (assuming you have the traditional model)?
	▪ How much time is consumed by all parties involved—employees, managers, HR teams, others?
	▪ What is the average time from the initiation of the process until it is complete?
	▪ What are the statistics—average rating, highest/lowest, number completed in a year, turnover rate, correlation between high performance and length of service, raises, etc.? How many managers have to complete them?

You may have already collected much of this data prior to pulling your design team together. If so, great. Just be sure to walk all of your team members through it so that everyone has the benefit of the insights you've collected. On the other hand, if you're just beginning to collect the data, dividing up the collection effort among the team is great way to get everyone involved and started on their own journey. While your design team will come to you with all sorts of views of their own, it is important for them to hear voices from each corner of your organization as well.

When I'm working with clients, it's at this point that we work with the design team to assess its organization's current performance management solution against best practices. To do so, we often use PeopleFirm's Talent Strategy Accelerator, a tool that helps teams explore both their current and desired states against a defined set of best practices. More than anything, we find that it ignites great conversations and gets the ideas flowing. There's no reason why you can't do something similar. Invite your design team to take a good hard look at what you're doing today and assess how it stands up to the basic premises of the

Fundamental Shifts. Simply walk through each of the eight shifts and discuss how well your current solution supports the ideas presented by the shift. You'll see a world of possibility open up before their eyes.

Before you exit this first step of the Sketch phase, pause for a moment with your design team to capture what you've collectively learned. Have the team members share their most important takeaways. Were there any surprises? Are there elements of what you're doing today that you don't want to lose? Are there things you can't wait to leave behind? Does the time and effort your organization is putting into the current process produce reasonable value for that effort? Does your process send the right message to your employees and managers? Is your approach to performance management helping you create your desired culture, or something completely opposite? Are there complexities within your organization that will need to be considered when you move into design? This hearty discussion about your current state will help your team understand how big a change you're shooting for and how change-ready your organization is.

SUPPORT AND BUY-IN CHECKPOINT

Remember, we want our wider ring of leaders, influencers, and naysayers to come with us on this journey. So pause here and share with them what you've learned. Don't assume that they know it; they probably don't. Help them begin to unstick their old thinking by sharing what you've heard—both what's working and what's not. Nothing helps break down assumptions and closed-minded attitudes better than exposing people to what others have said, are thinking, and care about. Where you can, anchor what you learn in the research, and blend that research with what you've learned about your own organization. Together, they'll make a powerful story.

Understand Your Organization's Destination

Now that you've grounded the design team in the here and now, it's time to shift your focus to the future. But before we can define our future performance solution, we need to agree on the future vision of the organization. After all, how can you build the best performance management solution, and one that's customized to your needs, if you're not clear on the future your organization is seeking? So that means getting your team totally aligned on what that future looks like. It may feel like spending this time is slowing you down when you are eager to jump into discussing options for your new performance management solution, but doing so will give you the credibility you need down the line because it's very hard for anyone to argue with a solution that is anchored in your corporate strategy. Many organizations miss this step, but believe me when I tell you that it can be the difference between a great design that addresses your unique organizational needs and a warmed-over performance solution that fits about as well as your grandpa's suit.

At PeopleFirm, we recognize that high-performing organizations optimize their impact and performance across the five key dimensions of Strategy, Culture, Structure, People, and Work. We'll use these five key dimensions as the framework by which you can test how well your design team agrees on the future of your organization and how that future should be reflected in your approach to performance management. For each of the disciplines, I've included a set of questions for your team to consider (see figure 6.2). My hope is that as your team achieves stronger understanding, clarity, and alignment on these questions, your design choices and tradeoffs regarding your performance solutions will take less effort and will be more effective at getting you to the right end state.

Figure 6.2. Understanding your organization's destination: Questions from the five dimensions of business.

Strategy	• What is the stated vision and mission of the organization? Is the destination clear, and does it connect with your people emotionally?
	• Will your business model or strategy change in the near future? If so, how will it change what's expected from your people?
	• Is there a clearly articulated strategic framework? Is it understood by your people? Does it influence how they perform their work?
	• Are key metrics established and shared? Do you anticipate being more metrics-driven in the future?
	• Are your competitors driving change in your industry? Will it increase competitiveness in the labor market for talent?

Culture	▪ What aspects of your current culture do you want to preserve/reinforce? ▪ Does your future include a change to your culture? If so, what are the key changes you are seeking? How significant is changing your PM approach to driving that culture change? ▪ What cultural elements should be emphasized in your approach to PM (e.g., innovation, collaboration, transparency)? ▪ What are the hidden drivers of culture that should be accounted for in the design process? ▪ What cultural influences exist or are anticipated (e.g., multicountry, leadership changes, acquisitions, etc.)?
Structure	▪ How is your organization structured? Will it change in the future? ▪ Does your future call for fewer silos and/or greater collaboration? ▪ How important is hierarchy today? Will it be the same in the future? ▪ Will informal reporting relationships be part of your structure as you evolve? ▪ Is there a need in the future for greater role clarity and/or enhanced consistency? Is PM expected to support that improved clarity? ▪ Are you looking to increase talent mobility across the organization? ▪ Do you expect the importance of teams to increase or change? ▪ How will structure influence your PM design; what constructs do you need to work within (business units, teams, or geographies)?
People	▪ What is the organizational philosophy on investing in talent? ▪ Do you have a defined talent strategy? If so, what is the role that PM will play in that strategy? How integrated will it be with other dimensions of your talent management solution? ▪ What will your talent mix look like in the next three, five, ten years? Are there risks you need to begin managing now? ▪ Do you need to address key shortages or needs to deliver on your vision? ▪ In the future, will your success be more dependent than it is now on your people having visibility into opportunities for development or advancement? ▪ What is the employee experience you want to provide for your people? ▪ What is the importance of increased talent analytics and insights?

Work	<ul><li>What are the key work processes that drive your strategy?</li><li>What attributes define the working environment (office environment versus teams in the field, virtual workface, etc.)? Will it change anytime soon?</li><li>How will teams collaborate in the future?</li><li>How will your employees capture and share knowledge in the future?</li><li>What relevant systems or tools do your teams use today? Tomorrow?</li><li>In the future, is there an opportunity to better integrate performance management with how people do their work?</li><li>Does your future include a focus on work/process simplification?</li><li>How will you measure (internal and external) customer satisfaction in the future? How will that influence your work?</li></ul>

Using the questions above as a guide, start by having your design team discuss and answer the questions as a group. Capture the key assumptions and points of view that you all have in common. Work out the differences and identify unresolved questions. Take those unresolved questions, as well as any other issues that arise, to the group of leaders you've invited into the conversation (or other people who can help). Ask for answers. Whenever you can, push people to be specific and test their views. Remember, your mission is to drive alignment in order to create the clarity you'll need to have a strong platform on which to build.

It's absolutely imperative that you reach strong agreement within your design team and among your key influencers about that shared vision for your organization and for performance management before you start building or, heaven forbid, implementing. A strong alignment of purpose is the best foundation you can possibly have. It's an asset that will pay off tenfold as you continue your journey.

> ## SUPPORT AND BUY-IN CHECKPOINT
>
> If your organization is like most, you've had to engage your leaders in this step of the process again and again as you dug into it. Why? Because too often these strategic questions are not clearly articulated. In fact, for many organizations, driving this conversation can be a meaningful added benefit of the process.
>
> If you've engaged a broader set of individuals in this conversation, be sure to communicate the conclusions and assumptions you will be building upon to your leaders, your HR team, and anyone else involved. Since these elements will highly influence your solution design, ensuring that they are well known and generally agreed upon is very important.

Creating Your Custom Design Principles

Here's where things really start to get fun. Just remember that the groundwork you've completed in the previous steps should leave you well prepared to make good choices as you go forward—choices anchored in the wisdom gained from your exploration of your past, present, and future. Not only are you wiser (if also a little older), but also I would hope that your design team is inspired to make a meaningful change for your people and your organization. In other words, with your team's knapsacks full of knowledge and inspiration, it's time to define, articulate, and validate your design principles.

Wait! What the heck are design principles? Well, let's talk about them: what they are and why they're important. Essentially, design principles are the guiding light for your new performance solution. They capture the fundamental goals and describe the desired attributes that are most important for your design. Design principles give your design team a means to gauge design decisions, and they provide a testing ground, if you will, when choosing between different approaches, options, and practices for your new performance management solution.

Let me give you a little illustration. Imagine that you and your significant other are getting ready to build a house. You've already purchased the lot and have selected the design/build contractor. Today you're preparing for your first meeting with the architect. Before the big meeting, the two of you go to lunch with the idea of settling on the attributes of the house that are most important to your family. You do this because you've decided it's best to be sure that you are both on the same page before you find yourselves saying yes to all of the architect's ideas. Why? Because you have a budget that you need to stay within. Hey, that right there—wanting to stick to a budget—is a design principle! You've already established one, and you're just getting started.

At lunch you both quickly agree that, yes, staying within budget is Design Principle #1. Then the debate begins over the other principles. You want four bedrooms: a master, two for the kids, and one for your parents, who you hope will spend more time with you in the future. Your spouse would prefer to stick with three bedrooms (while carefully avoiding stating an opinion about the prospect of increased visits from the in-laws) and would like to add a home office. In the end, the two of you define the key elements that are musts for your future house. You may even prioritize them.

You'll notice that at this point in the process you're not picking countertops and plumbing fixtures; you're dealing only with those bigger items that will drive the structure and usability of the house, like rooms, square footage, and budget. Later, as the house design process evolves, you'll find comfort in returning to your prioritized design principles. They become your anchor for making tradeoff decisions and give you the courage to say no to any extra bells and whistles that might tempt you along the way. In other words, your design principles keep you true to your priorities.

It's no different when you're building a performance management process. These design principles will capture your big-picture priorities and provide an anchor to keep you on track when you're assessing new options and ideas. They offer a great way to test your design, serving as a check-in to see that you've stayed the course and haven't reverted back to old thinking or been wooed away by sexy ideas or tools. (Don't laugh; this happens all too often, and yes, there are sexy design tools. At least we in the consulting world think there are.) The design principles also give you an easy way to validate your intent with others, such as those influential leaders you want to keep with you on the journey. I find that the design principles are one of the best places to start when you need to describe your solution, as they provide clarity on why certain philosophies, methods, tools, and features became part of your end solution.

Creating your unique design principles should be fairly easy once your team is tuned in and ready to roll (and it should be, by this point). When you gather your design team to create your design principles, I recommend starting with a quick review of what you've learned from the previous steps. In short, talk with your team about the journey thus far. Reflect on the big lessons from both the current state activities and the future vision work. Then get your team started by asking them the questions in figure 6.3.

Figure 6.3. Design principle questions.

Overall	■ What's the most important outcome? ■ Success means your employees will describe the solution as _____? ■ Success means your managers will describe the solution as _____? ■ The biggest change the team will experience is _____? ■ What will stay the same?
Develop People	■ How will your solution inspire great careers? ■ What words describe the employee experience you will create or reinforce? ■ What three words will describe giving or receiving feedback? ■ What talent challenges or needs do you want your solution to help solve?
Reward Equitably	■ What three words should describe your proposed rewards philosophy? ■ What behaviors do you most want to reward? ■ How will rewards be determined in the future?
Drive Organizational Performance	■ What strategic goals or imperatives will be supported through your solution? ■ What role will the solution play in connecting individuals and teams to the vision, strategy, or operational plans? ■ Name the top three cultural norms you wish to reinforce or introduce. (Is there one or more you're wanting to eliminate?)

The trick to articulating great design principles is making them crisp and well-defined. You want each principle to both stand on its own and collectively capture the vision of your solution. And you don't want the list to be too long. I usually shoot for five to eight at most. Above all, these design principles should capture the macro ideas and intent (like the fact that it needs to be employee-driven), and not dip down into the features, mechanics, or tools of the solution (such as how employees will communicate their development goals). In other words, they should be about how many rooms you want, not what tile you'll use in the shower. We'll get to those flashy finish details soon, I promise.

⚒ CREATING YOUR CUSTOM DESIGN PRINCIPLES

How do you help your team brainstorm these principles? You may have a facilitation process that works for you and your organization; if so, forge ahead with that. If, on the other hand, you'd like my step-by-step, nitty-gritty recommendation for facilitating the creation of your design principles, check out "Creating Your Custom Design Principles" in the Toolbox.

SUPPORT AND BUY-IN CHECKPOINT

This is a great time to touch base with the design team members individually. Ask them if they are happy with the process. Are they excited about the changes that the team is driving? What concerns do they have? Do they feel their voices are adequately represented in the work to date? What else should the design team be doing to create a successful outcome?

And, by the way, it's not a bad time to send a quick note to your team members' supervisors thanking them again for lending their valuable people to your efforts.

Sketch Your Frame against the Three Common Goals

Now that you have created your design principles, I find it incredibly helpful to double-check your team's thinking by looking at how they align with the Three Common Goals. One fun way to do this is by using the visual aid of our performance management triangle, or frame, described in chapter 4. This provides a visual representation of your decisions and allows you to test which direction your design is leaning. In the Toolbox, I've provided you with a set of worksheets and instructions for completing your sketching process. (Additional worksheets can be downloaded at **www.thePMReboot.com**.)

⚒ DESIGN PRINCIPLE WORKSHEET AND SKETCHPAD

Begin with the "Design Principle Worksheet," which calculates the three points on your frame and weighs how well each of your design principles supports the Three Common Goals, based on your priorities and your team's assessment. Then move on to the "Design Principle Sketchpad" to sketch your frame. Grab a trusty no. 2 pencil, pull up the worksheet, and start sketching. (Don't worry, there are more detailed instructions in the Toolbox.) Once you've sketched your frame, come on back here.

How does it look? Does the shape of your frame represent the outcome you expected? Do you have one goal that you're hoping to emphasize? Is it clear that your design principles will deliver impact in the area of desired emphasis? For instance, let's say your aim is to focus much more on developing your people. Does your frame lean toward *develop people* (meaning that the *develop people* score is farther out on its axis)?

If you complete your sketch and see that it isn't representing the structure you thought you were building, it may inspire your team to fine-tune your design principles. For example, your sketch may show that your frame is leaning toward reward equitably, although your team firmly believes they've been putting the emphasis on develop people. To adjust for this discrepancy, you may agree to change the priorities within your design principle list, or edit the language you used to articulate those principles to confirm that the list accurately reflects your underlying intent and thinking.

If you were to complete this same worksheet with your current process, what would it look like when it was sketched out? What do you think is the biggest shift between the two? Does that shift seem reasonable, given what your design team has been thinking about the differences between where you are today and where you want to go? Discuss among yourselves. Adjust if need be. And sketch it again until you feel it is right.

Sketching your frame also helps you make decisions about the interconnectedness—or the lack thereof—among the Three Common Goals. The connectedness of your solution is a pretty darned important design consideration and should not be overlooked. Now is the perfect point in your process to discuss those connections with your team.

When we talk about connectedness, we're talking about how the lines between the three points of your frame look. In real life, we're talking about how related you expect your design to be across the three goals. For example, if you'd like to connect your base pay directly to a capabilities model by job family (say, creating four engineering levels ranging from apprentice to journeyman), then you're drawing a strong connection between *develop people* and *reward equitably,* since the only way for an engineer to earn an increase in pay is to increase his or her skills and capabilities. When sketching, I'd represent that with a thick, bold line to show that these two are strongly connected, as in figure 6.4.

Figure 6.4. Example connection from *reward equitably* to *develop people.*

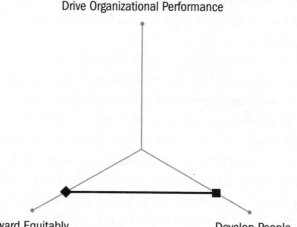

Drive Organizational Performance

Reward Equitably   Develop People

Now let's say that you've decided to separate employee development conversations from the annual goal-setting process, in which all employees define personal goals in support of the company's strategic plan. That said, even though they've been uncoupled, you recognize that as people develop their skills and capabilities, organizational performance is likely to be enhanced. This, then, would indicate a light connection between *drive organizational performance* and *develop people,* and you might represent that with a dashed line, as in figure 6.5.

Figure 6.5. Example connection from *drive organizational performance* to *develop people*.

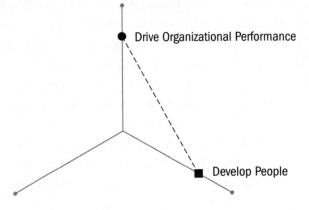

See where I'm going with this? In these two examples, I've used a thick, bold line to show the strong connections between the goals and a dashed line to indicate a very light connection.

Go back and take a look at your sketch, and get your team discussing the linkages. Draw thick lines to show what's strongly connected, and make thinner lines to show less of a connection. You may even eliminate the line(s) completely for elements that are going to be handled independently. Refine your lines until they reflect your thinking. Don't sweat it if the three points aren't connected, assuming that the lack of connection fits your needs. And don't worry if you're not sure about how a connection should look. There is no right answer, so you can't get it wrong. This is an art, not a science, and the value of considering the type of line you might use to show the connections is mostly in the conversation that the sketching will drive and the insights you gain from seeing a visual representation of how your design is shaping up.

✖ CROWDSOURCING YOUR DESIGN PRINCIPLES

When you're in the process of defining your design principles, you might wish you could invite people beyond your design team to weigh in and provide their views on the top priorities for your future performance solution. This may be especially true if you have key influencers within your organization with notably divergent views on the topic. How great would it be if you could start the dialogue with a diverse team, yet know the preferred design principles of each person? What if you could assess their design principles against the Three Common Goals and see what kind of performance management frame each person would design if she were left to her own devices? Even better, right? Not only would you be able to compare their perspectives, but you would have a great way to start a conversation that could help build alignment across the group.

I have a little shortcut that will allow contributors to sketch their ideas in ten minutes or less. Even the busiest of executives can't argue with that. Check out the Toolbox section "Crowdsourcing Your Design Principles," where I provide more insight into the value of this approach and the link to our online tool.

SUPPORT AND BUY-IN CHECKPOINT

Now that you've tested your principles and perhaps made a few adjustments, socialize them before you move on to configuration. Your sponsoring executives and influential leaders are key, but you may also want to expand your reach to the conversation group you engaged earlier in the process. If you've prepared well, it's unlikely that you'll get feedback that demands big changes; minor adjustments are far more likely, and, in fact, they're to be expected.

At this point in the process, you want to shift away from gathering information from your people to sharing information about what has informed your solution. Build awareness, understanding, and ultimately support by sharing this cool new thing you've built with their feedback. The people outside your design team have not been absorbed in this effort as deeply as you have, so you may need to back up now and then to remind them why you're driving this change, point out how traditional models have failed us, and refresh them on a few of the shifts that need to be considered to achieve your goals. A key change management tenet to live by: meet them where they are!

Chapter 7

CONFIGURE YOUR SOLUTION

Mobilize

Plan, invite participants, and get started

Sketch

Align on your principles of design

Configure

Configure, test, and validate your solution

Build

Build your solution, manage dependencies

Implement

Plan the change, implement, and evaluate

OK, SO YOUR TEAM HAS AGREED to your design principles and you're ready to roll. This means we now leave Sketch and shift into the Configure phase. Why "Configure"? Because this stage is all about selecting the practices, options, and features that will best match your design principles and bring your solution to life. Yep, we're finally choosing plumbing fixtures and cabinet door styles!

When configuring, you'll define a portfolio of **PM Practices** that together will make up your complete solution. PM Practices are tangible methods, practices, tools, and activities that together create your unique approach to driving organizational performance, developing people, and rewarding equitably in a manner consistent with your design principles. The list of potential PM Practices is long, but a few examples might include setting quarterly goals tied to a defined rewards model, creating development plans, or introducing a formal mentoring program. Some of these PM Practices may be new, meaning that you'll be introducing them to the organization. Others may be practices that are already in use, which you decide to keep because they work well and because they support your design principles. During configuration we will also define the attributes that establish "who," "when," and "how" for each PM Practice. So if you happen to choose formal mentoring as a desired future PM Practice, during configuration you'll define who will participate in the mentoring, when mentoring activities are expected to occur, and how people will engage in the mentoring process.

Configuration is where you take all of the exploration, learnings, thinking, ideas, and design discussions that have come from your early work and apply that knowledge and insight to creating your future performance solution. You'll start this phase by simply brainstorming PM Practices and selecting those that best meet your needs. Then, before you dig into configuring each of the PM Practices, you'll quickly confirm that you're on track against your design principles and that you haven't missed any important practices. Once you're confident in your selections, you'll define each practice in more detail to understand how each will work when implemented. Before leaving configuration, you'll test your design to see how you did against your design principles and the Three Common Goals. Rigorous? Yes, but it's important work, so let's get to it.

Brainstorm

This is the fun part! There is nothing better than sitting in a room with your team (or a virtual room, as the case may be), all in agreement on where you want to go and getting ready to figure out how to arrive there. Now is the time to start dreaming up all the ways you can achieve your aims for your new performance management solution!

I commented a few paragraphs back that the list of PM Practices is long. Why is this? Because, as you know, performance management covers a lot of territory, as in our Three Common Goals; multiple employee segments; and a huge range of employee expectations and needs across thousands of unique organizations. So, given the fact that we have a long list of options and ideas, I find that it helps to consider them by category. I like to use these six categories: Goals and Alignment, Feedback and Performance Insight, Coaching and Mentoring, Career and Development Planning, Talent Reviews and Insights, and Total Rewards (see figure 7.1). I find that these six categories represent the primary areas of focus for most PM Practices; however, you're free to add, remove, or change categories to fit the unique needs and goals of your organization.

Begin by discussing your ideas for each category. I like to put each category on a flip chart to record ideas. It's at this time that I find many of the ideas and discussions that came up in the previous steps of Redesign will begin to jell.

Figure 7.1. Facilitation example.

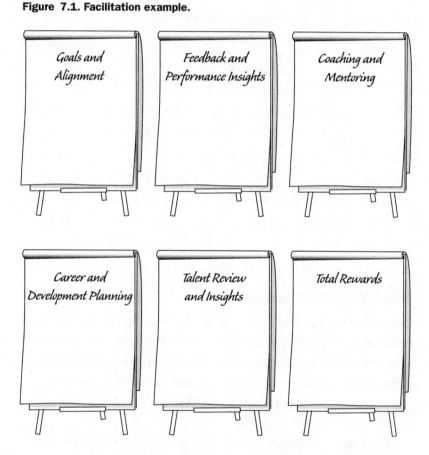

These don't have to be full-fledged PM Practices at this point; keep things loose, and just capture your ideas, thoughts, and perspectives. Refrain from critiquing or debating while you get the ideas flowing. However, you do want to stay true to your design principles! To be honest, that usually isn't a problem; at this point, I find that most teams are so committed to their design principles that they won't even think of putting forward an idea that doesn't fit them. It would be like talking about what sort of pizza oven you want when your design principle calls for a simple, inexpensive kitchen. Figure 7.2 provides an example of how your brainstorm might look:

Figure 7.2. Example: Feedback and Performance Insights.

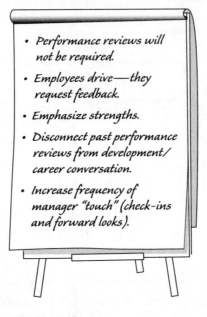

- *Performance reviews will not be required.*
- *Employees drive—they request feedback.*
- *Emphasize strengths.*
- *Disconnect past performance reviews from development/ career conversation.*
- *Increase frequency of manager "touch" (check-ins and forward looks).*

Select Your PM Practices

Once your team has exhausted its brainstorming reserves, it's time to get down to the business of selecting the actual PM Practices that will make up your performance solution. This selection step is a forcing function, driving you to distill those brainstormed ideas into specific **methods, practices, tools,** or **activities** that will deliver on your design principles and bring your full solution to life.

I recommend starting at the top of the six categories. Walk through each one, review your ideas, and then select or define a PM Practice that will best deliver on those ideas. (Be sure to take good notes on the nuances of the PM Practices you're choosing, as those details are likely to influence your choices in the configuration step that is coming up soon.) If we use the Feedback and Performance Insights example above, you might summarize the ideas captured there into three specific PM Practices:

1. No formal reviews required, frequent manager check-ins are expected.

2. Employees may request written feedback (optional).

3. Strengths-based development discussions on six-month cadence—scheduled by employee.

CONFIGURATION CHECKLIST

To help you close any possible gaps in your design, I've provided a "Configuration Checklist" in the Toolbox. This is a list of potential PM Practice options for your team to consider; check it against your list to see if you've missed anything or if it triggers any more great ideas. Again, start at the top of your list and walk through each one. Is there anything within any category that your team should add to your design?

SUPPORT AND BUY-IN CHECKPOINT

A final word before you move on: Be brave! Fear of change can derail you even at this late stage. Teams often start out boldly defining their design principles, excited about the future possibilities. They start the configuration process ready to create something new, thoughtful, and effective. But as they begin to walk through specific choices, tough decisions emerge, such as walking away from formal reviews, or trusting and empowering managers to determine rewards.

As the realities of these PM Practice choices sink in, teams often falter. Why? Because these choices represent breaking with tradition or challenging the ideas we were raised to believe. Fear and doubt creep in as we start to wonder, "What will our executives think? Can we trust our managers? Are we really confident that this will work?" I've watched teams leap forward and then fall back as they wrestled with these decisions. In fact, you should expect that you will go three steps forward and one back. It's the normal tension that's inherent in letting go and driving change. Honestly, this is the hardest part of rebooting. As long as you continue to move forward and make the best choices for your organization, things will work out. Keep calm and carry on!

Confirm That You've Got It Covered

My experience has shown that at this point most teams are about 80 percent of the way there with their selected PM Practices. Now I want to help you over the finish line by confirming your PM Practice selections, scanning for conflicts and redundancies, and making sure that you didn't miss anything along the way.

To confirm your design choices, take a look at the PM Practices you've selected, and consider how they are or aren't supporting each of the Three Common Goals *(develop people, reward equitably, and drive organizational performance)*. Have you selected practices that will deliver on your intent? Do they support your design principles? For instance, if you decided that you want to put a heavy emphasis on developing people, check to make sure that your options reflect that priority. Are there any redundancies or conflicts in your design? Have you overbuilt, added too much? Maybe you need to narrow down the selected practices and streamline your solution. Spend a little time in discussion with your team, and gauge your level of confidence in what you've selected and defined so far. Remember, it's perfectly fine (in fact, it might be great) to pick a PM Practice for a single targeted employee segment rather than only ones that fit all the employees within your scope. Customization decisions of this nature are often what drive additions during this confirmation step.

Configure Your PM Practices

In this step, your mission is to decide what each of your chosen PM Practices is going to look like in the real world—in other words, *how* it will be implemented in your organization. I've found that in order to understand how these practices will show up in your organization, we first need to define four parameters: participants (scope), timing (cadence and frequency), ownership, and assessment. As an example, take "Frequent manager check-ins for all employees": Who will it affect? How often is "frequent"? Whose responsibility is it? And how will you know it's being done? Defining these four parameters brings the design to life by capturing the essence of who, when, where, and a bit of the how. It might help to consider the questions in figure 7.3.

Figure 7.3. PM Practices configuration questions.

PM PRACTICES CONFIGURATION QUESTIONS	
Participants	▪ What employee groups will be in the scope of the option you've selected? ▪ Are there unique groups or segments that will be managed differently from others? (e.g., top performers, functions, by level)
Timing	▪ Frequency: How often will this activity occur? ▪ Cadence: Will timing be the same for all people (say, calendar based), or will other triggers drive the activity, such as an anniversary?
Ownership	▪ Who owns the initiation of the process? ▪ Is there a formal signing off? If so, who owns it? ▪ Who's involved? Do others have a role, such as peers or team members?

Assessment	▪ Will there be an assessment element? If so, formal or informal?
	
	▪ Will there be a rating? If so:
	
	  ▪ At what level is a score assigned? (By goal, behavior, etc.)
	
	  ▪ Is there an expected distribution?

Continuing in the spirit of showing rather than telling, let's consider the process of configuring two similar PM Practices: informal mentoring and formal mentoring. As shown in figures 7.4 and 7.5, we are configuring each by defining the details within the four parameters. This example demonstrates how these two similar PM Practices will be different when executed. For example, informal mentoring has a broad scope (participants = all employees), but formal mentoring is limited to the HIPO (high potentials) audience. For the three other parameters, our configuration notes show that there will be less structure, which is in keeping with the nature of informal mentoring. On the other hand, formal mentoring requires more rigor in the way it will be managed internally, with a defined schedule of events and owners accountable for making it happen. So you see how two PM Practices that might seem quite similar in their unconfigured states actually end up being very different once you've defined their parameters. As demonstrated by this example, the choices you make when configuring the parameters can make a huge difference in what your new solution will look like in the end.

Figure 7.4. Configuration example: Informal mentoring.

CONFIGURATION CATEGORY	PM PRACTICE	PARTICIPANTS/ SCOPE	TIMING	OWNERSHIP	ASSESSMENT
Feedback and Performance Insights 	Informal mentoring	All employees	Ad hoc— as driven by mentee	■ Mentees drive process. ■ HR to facilitate mentor connections. ■ Career champions to advocate usage of mentoring.	None

Figure 7.5. Configuration example: Formal mentoring.

CONFIGURATION CATEGORY	PM PRACTICE	PARTICIPANTS/ SCOPE	TIMING	OWNERSHIP	ASSESSMENT
Talent Reviews and Insights 	Formal mentoring	HIPOs	Quarterly meetings	■ Mentors drive process. ■ HR assigns mentors.	Quality of relationship assessed yearly.

PM PRACTICES CONFIGURATION TEMPLATE

Your turn to configure! To help you in the process, I've created the PM Practices Configuration Template to capture your results. You'll find this with our other online tools at **www.thePMReboot.com**. Once your worksheet is completed, the rows will look something like those in figure 7.6.

Figure 7.6. Example of Configuration Rows.

CONFIGURATION CATEGORY	PM PRACTICE	PARTICIPANTS/ SCOPE	TIMING	OWNERSHIP	ASSESSMENT
Talent Reviews and Insights	■ Talent review to identify differentiated performance and increase visibility of top talent	■ High potential employees ■ Employees with critical skills	■ Frequency: Annually ■ Cadence: Staggered by practice area	■ Owner: Practice or interest leaders ■ Facilitator: HR business partners ■ Involve: All people managers	■ Groups into three categories (high/med/low) ■ Succession and stretch projects considered ■ No forced distribution

How did it go? I assume you were able to achieve even greater clarity on your design as you defined the parameters of each PM Practice. If so, it's time for a group hug. You've done it! You've designed your spanking-new, totally custom, cutting-edge performance management solution. Mission accomplished, right? Well, almost . . .

SUPPORT AND BUY-IN CHECKPOINT

You've just completed a big milestone. In fact, this was the nut of what you've been pining to do all along, right? I'm guessing that you and the team are excited about your solution. And you should be. But before you run out the door waving your configuration table around, read on. Follow the step that I'll outline in the next section to test your design before validating your approach and building support outside the design team.

If configuration raised some questions, then sure, go seek some answers. Do a bit of your own testing prior to asking others to look at your baby with a critical eye.

Test Your Configuration

Now it's time to test that design of yours, but how? It's as simple as going back and assessing how well you've designed your solution in accordance with your prioritized and articulated design principles.

Post your prioritized design principles on the wall (write them on a whiteboard or flip chart, or print them out as a big poster—whatever suits your team). Then work down the list of practices, rating how well your solution meets each design principle. (Yes, it's OK to rate a solution. It's far better than rating people!) I personally like using Harvey balls (those little circle graphs they use in *Consumer Reports*) to create a visual assessment, as shown in figure 7.7, but use whatever scoring system you like best. What matters here is that you look critically at how well you've picked your PM Practices and configured your solution in support of your validated design principles.

Figure 7.7 Testing PM Practices alignment to design principles.

PRIORITY	DESIGN PRINCIPLE	HOW STRONGLY DOES OUR SOLUTION DELIVER ON THIS PRINCIPLE?
1	Align our global team to our vision and goals	●
2	Encourage collaboration and knowledge sharing organization-wide	◕
3	Provide insight into global talent pools by areas of practice	●
4	Align base pay to capabilities, reward for client growth and impact	●
5	Build global account capabilities and leaders	◕
6	Fuel innovation and service advancement	◑
7	Increase focus on client delivery satisfaction	◑

Next, discuss your scores among the design team. Are you happy with how your solution meets the design principles? If it isn't scoring as well as you'd like, think about whether it's missing a key element, or if perhaps it's just out of balance (meaning some design principles are emphasized too much, while others are not supported enough). If necessary, go back to the configuration step, and tune your design options to better deliver on your intent. Your goal is to verify that the solution design is striking the right balance to deliver on your promises to the organization.

After looking at each design principle, pull back and assess your overall solution. Discuss these questions among your team:

- Will our solution meet our expectations and the expectations we've created within the organization?

- Will our solution create the employee experience and deliver the organizational insights we've planned for?

- Have we stayed true to our intent, or fallen back into old thinking or safer waters?

⚒ Configuration Worksheet and Sketchpad

For the benefit of process nerds like me, I'll give you one more way to test your design: resketch your frame, testing your configured solution against the Three Common Goals. Remember, last time you were sketching based on your design principles. If your configured solution is true to your design principles, this new sketch should resemble your first. If this isn't the case, then the differences should initiate some healthy discussion among your design team about whether you've tilted your focus too far in one direction or another or simply weren't bold enough in your choices. You'll find full directions on conducting this second test, along with a Configuration Worksheet and a Configuration Sketchpad, in the Toolbox.

Are these tests an exact science? Not at all. But each provides a means to test your design—and build your team's confidence in it—before you move on. This is your design: If it's not where you want it to be yet, fix it. If it is, celebrate the hard work and the progress you've made, and ready the team for the next steps to making it a reality.

SUPPORT AND BUY-IN CHECKPOINT

Earlier I suggested that you hold off on sharing your design with the organization at large until you've had a chance to test it within your team and with your design principles in mind. But now that you've thoroughly tested your solution, you may be ready to shop it around to validate your thinking and test the readiness of the organization. If you do, please be sure to tell the full story. It's easy to forget that you've been in on every step of this journey but others have not. Again, you want to meet people where they are.

I know you are ready to talk solution, but it is quite likely that others may still be asking, "Why are we taking this on now? What's wrong with what we're doing today? What are you trying to accomplish, anyway?" So start at the beginning, and walk them through the story of why you're changing, how your destination has influenced your thinking, what your design principles are, and the manner in which you intend to deliver on those principles. For many, this will not be the first time they've heard it, but it's still valuable for the folks who were invited to the conversation to be reminded of the path you've taken and why the journey was necessary in the first place.

Chapter 8

MAKING IT REAL

NEED A LITTLE BREATHER AFTER ALL THE WORK WE'VE
DONE? Well, sit back, relax, and let me tell you a few stories.

Up to now, we've been working in the realm of the hypothetical,
and the picture can get pretty fuzzy without some tangible examples
to solidify our understanding of the process and results. If you can't
visualize the way your solution will play out in the everyday work of
your organization, then you're going to be dead in the water. To help
you convert that theory into everyday action, let's take a look at how all
this information I've thrown at you has played out for a few different
organizations. These how-they-did-it stories involve composites of
real companies that PeopleFirm has worked with in the past few years
and should give you a feel for how performance management can be
successfully rebooted, while also providing some helpful tips that you
might be able to apply as you create your own story.

I'll begin by introducing you to a company I'm going to call Peace.org.

Story #1: Peace.org

THE STARTING PLACE. Peace.org is a nonprofit. Like many nonprofits,
they are big on purpose but perpetually short on funds. Because the
majority of their employees come to them feeling a connection to the
mission of the organization, turnover has historically been low despite
the low pay and long hours. However, in recent months they've lost a
few of their key people to peer organizations. Another big change has
occurred over the summer as well: the longstanding managing director
has retired and has been replaced by a new leader.

THE DESTINATION. The new managing director was tasked by the board to double the impact that the organization is having across the globe. To meet this audacious goal, the organization is going to have to perform at a higher level than ever before, especially since doubling the impact does not mean doubling the resources. In the past, Peace.org had tried to force a corporate model of performance management onto the organization, based on the recommendation of a vocal board member. It failed miserably within their culture, and a set of the review templates literally became a dartboard in the break room. Understanding this history (since it was quite willingly shared by many of the team, and hey, the dartboard was evidence sitting right there in the break room), the new managing director decided that he needed to look for a new approach to increase performance and improve the retention of their key talent. He also recognized that funding would continue to be tight, so pay increases were not a viable option in the near future.

PEACE.ORG'S DESIGN PRINCIPLES AND FRAME. After working through the design process, the design team at Peace.org created their five design principles and determined that their frame should look something like the one in figure 8.1. Not surprisingly, their frame shows that they are high in *drive organizational performance* and *develop people—* the two key goals that the managing director wanted most to support.

The Peace.org team decided on the following design principles:

The new performance management solution will . . .

1. Increase every employee's connection to our mission

2. Engage the full team in setting operational goals

3. Reinforce our culture code

4. Create mastery in all areas of our organization

5. Be simple and effective without getting in the way

Figure 8.1. Peace.org's frame.

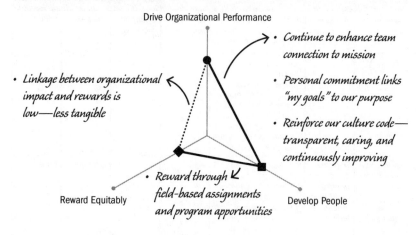

PEACE.ORG'S CONFIGURATION. As the team dug into configuring their solution, they made the choices shown in figure 8.2:

Figure 8.2. Configuration example: Peace.org.

CONFIGURATION CATEGORY	PM PRACTICE	DESIGN NOTES	PARTICIPANTS	TIMING	OWNERSHIP	ASSESSMENT
Goals and Alignment	Collaborative strategic planning	■ Engage employees in annual strategy development and quarterly reviews to increase their personal connection ■ Openly discuss operational strategies, investment, and tradeoffs with the team	All employees	Annual planning, quarterly team reviews	Managing director	Team performance against goals
	Personal commitment statements	■ Employees will write personal commitment statements in a short "this is why I'm here and what I'm hoping to accomplish this year" declaration.	All employees	Completed annually, shared throughout year	Employee	None
Feedback and Performance Insights	Peer recognition	■ Weekly Friday wrap-up sessions will include call-outs for great work.	All employees	Weekly and ad hoc	Team	None
	Enhance continuous improvement culture and habits	■ Project management methodology will include discussions at key milestones and close-out sessions to seek continuous improvement.	All employees	Project dependent	Project leads	None
	Employee-driven feedback	■ Individuals are encouraged to seek feedback on how they are doing.	All employees	When sought	Employee	None

CONFIGURATION CATEGORY	PM PRACTICE	DESIGN NOTES	PARTICIPANTS	TIMING	OWNERSHIP	ASSESSMENT
Coaching and Mentoring	Manager engagement guidelines	■ Managers will have bimonthly one-on-one check-ins with their people. Resources will be created to support managers in these conversations (e.g., a list of possible conversation topics, questions to ask that align with commitments, and techniques for conflict resolution).	All employees	Bimonthly check-ins	Managers	None
Career and Development Planning	Employee-driven planning captured in commitments	■ Employees encouraged to go deep or wide, either to build mastery in selected area or expand nature of roles and work they can perform across the organization. They should outline their career aspirations and experiences in the commitments.	All employees	Completed annually, shared throughout the year	Employee	None
	Program assignment selection process	■ Careful assignment of programs is key driver and tactic of the development of skills and capabilities through real-life experience.	All employees	Driven by programs	Managing director	None
Talent Reviews and Insights	Annual staffing plans include workforce review, planned assignments, and capability need assessment	■ A staffing strategy will be developed in support of annual strategic planning. ■ Planned advancement and career moves are mapped out to support organization's needs and employee's aspirations. ■ New needs for organization or enhanced capabilities within the team are noted (connects to the recruiting plan and the assignment of programs to people).	All employees	Aligned with strategic plan and adapted as driven by programs	Managing director and senior team	N/A

CONFIGURATION CATEGORY	PM PRACTICE	DESIGN NOTES	PARTICIPANTS	TIMING	OWNERSHIP	ASSESSMENT
Total Rewards	Salary strategy review	▪ Focus is to keep salaries parallel to cost-of-living changes and in line with similar roles at peer organizations.	All employees	Employee anniversary review	HR/ Operations	Peer bench-marking
	Anniversary review	▪ Employees meet with managing director annually to review role, check in on how they're doing, and share expectations for future.	All employees	Employee anniversary review	Managing director	N/A
	Board-sponsored perks	▪ Board provides periodic recognition for key milestones, etc.	All employees	Ad hoc, event driven	Board	N/A
	Program assign-ments	▪ Since money is scarce, leaders will seek other ways to recognize and reward. With a focus on development, a top reward is offering field-based assignments and program opportunities to recognize great work and contributions (e.g., chance to work in Africa, something very meaningful to this team).	All employees	Driven by programs	Managing director	N/A

MY FAVORITE PM PRACTICE. The PM Practice that has been the biggest hit with the Peace.org team is the commitment process. Employees like it because they get the time and opportunity to explain their personal connection to the mission and how they want to grow with the organization, and leaders like it because they get to know more about how employees see themselves as part of the team (see figure 8.3). Each month during the all-hands meeting, two or three of the team members share their commitment with the group and talk about how things are going, what more they hope to do, and what they need from others to achieve their own aspirations. Over the past few years, the nature of the commitments has gotten more creative and taken on greater meaning within the organization.

Figure 8.3. Peace.org commitment postcard.

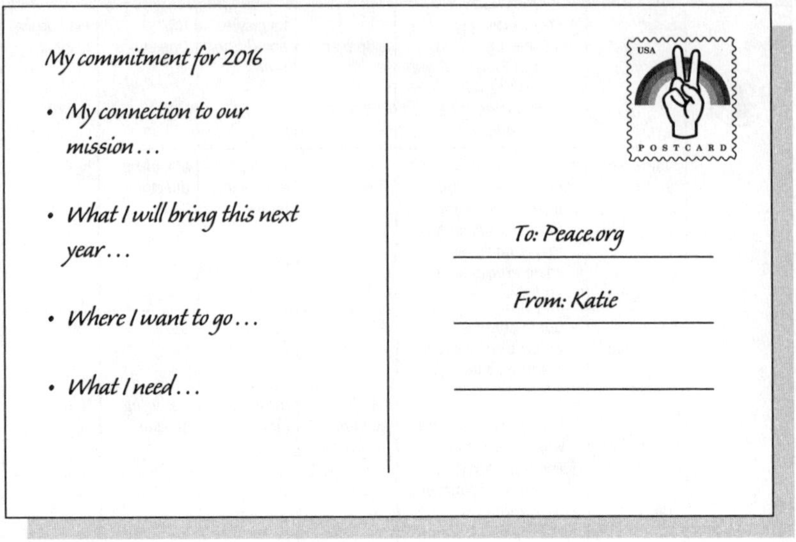

My commitment for 2016

- *My connection to our mission . . .*

- *What I will bring this next year . . .*

- *Where I want to go . . .*

- *What I need . . .*

To: Peace.org

From: Katie

The Nature of Nonprofits

Research shows that nonprofit organizations often struggle when trying to apply for-profit performance models to their own, very different, organizations.[1] Let's take a look at why this misses the mark.

Defining performance

Organizational performance in the nonprofit sector is often hard to define. For-profit organizations can use a clear bottom line as both their reason for existence and their performance measurement. In contrast, nonprofit organizations are often built around varied and complex missions, making it difficult to define an obvious measurement of success. Since mission achievement is not typically tied directly to the organization's ability to generate income, natural performance measures are rarely in place.

Cultural resistance

While nonprofit organizations are increasingly recognizing the need to bring more "business" practices into the management approach, many nonprofits resist these changes on a cultural level. And there's nothing that is more "corporate" than a traditional performance program. Interesting research from the University of Georgia notes that "there is a high degree of idealism within the nonprofit sector and reluctance among nonprofit employees to acknowledge that they are involved in competitive, market-based activities, and, for ideological reasons, they are reluctant to use market analysis."[2]

Having worked with a lot of nonprofit organizations, I've often experienced these struggles firsthand. But here's the thing: the focus on measurement is less critical if we can unite those groups of passionate people to work collaboratively toward a compelling and shared goal. In fact, the idealism prevalent in nonprofits can be a huge strength (or a significant weakness, depending on how well it's captured and leveraged). The strength of the idealism is realized when your performance design effectively taps into each individual's connection to the mission. But that idealism can become debilitating if you introduce performance approaches that are perceived as being a distraction from productive work or contrary to the mission.

With these ideas in mind, here are a few tips for designing performance solutions for the nonprofit environment:

- Keep it simple: research has shown that the success of a system of nonprofit measures is directly proportional to its simplicity.[3]

- Heavily emphasize the role of the mission in your solution design.

- Clearly define strategies or actions that will help your team bridge the gap between the lofty mission and your near-term goals and needs.

- When looking for metrics, consider impact, the level of activity, and outcomes related to your program mission and purpose.

- Be creative with reward strategies. Understand what motivates the people in your organization. (Tip: it's unlikely that pay is their top driver.)

- Don't try to force models that are contrary to the culture or mission.

Story #2: Services.com

THE STARTING PLACE. Services.com is a global consulting firm and a great example for other professional services organizations, like consulting, engineering, legal, or accounting. The rhythm of their business is based on project cycles, and their main asset, their differentiator, is their people. Because it is all about their people, development and retention are very important. Services.com has multiple offices scattered across North America, many of which were added over the years by acquiring other smaller firms. Recently they've also expanded into Europe, with new offices in the UK, France, and Germany.

THE DESTINATION. The global head of people (GHP) recently participated in the development of the five-year strategy for the firm. The vision is to meet the needs of global clients while continuing to grow services revenue and expand the firm's location footprint. Accomplishing this vision will require Services.com to create a more cohesive culture, increase the collaboration among their far-flung offices, and bring consistency to their methodologies, tools, and services within all key areas of practice. The GHP has outlined a set of talent initiatives to support this strategy. First out of that gate is reimaging their performance approach, since the company's long history of acquisitions has rendered the current one uneven.

SERVICES.COM'S DESIGN PRINCIPLES AND FRAME. The GHP has built a design team that gives her a diversity of experience, culture, and background by blending resources from multiple offices, representatives from each legacy firm acquired, and people from each of their practice areas, as well as a few representatives from headquarters. Here's how the team defined their design principles and PM frame, which you'll notice is relatively balanced across all three design goals (see figure 8.4).

The Services.com team decided on the following design principles:

The new performance management solution will . . .

1. Align our global team to our vision and goals

2. Encourage collaboration and knowledge sharing organization-wide

3. Provide insight into global talent pools by areas of practice

4. Align base pay to capabilities, rewards for client growth and impact

5. Build global account capabilities and leaders

6. Fuel innovation and service advancement

7. Increase focus on client delivery satisfaction

Figure 8.4. Services.com's frame.

SERVICES.COM'S CONFIGURATION. And the direction in which they took their solution is shown in figure 8.5.

Figure 8.5. Configuration example: Services.com.

CONFIGURATION CATEGORY	PM PRACTICE	DESIGN NOTES	PARTICIPANTS	TIMING	OWNERSHIP	ASSESSMENT
Goals and Alignment	Individuals share team goals and targets.	▪ To bring the global team together, all employees with the firm for more than a year will participate in a profit-sharing program based on set of team targets. ▪ Team goals established by geography, global account, and service area. ▪ Company targets and finances are shared openly with all employees each month.	All employees with >12 months' tenure	Semiannual	Team leaders	Team metrics and targets

CONFIGURATION CATEGORY	PM PRACTICE	DESIGN NOTES	PARTICIPANTS	TIMING	OWNERSHIP	ASSESSMENT
Goals and Alignment (continued)	Project-based shared agreements	▪ Rather than an annual cycle, Services.com opted for project-based agreements. These are commitments made by each individual assigned to a project. ▪ Shared agreements revolve around the project plans and create a shared contract between the project manager and the employee. ▪ Early in a project, employees meet with the project lead to discuss what needs to get done, what kind of experience they want out of this project, and how they want to work together.	All employees	Start of project, updated at key milestones or as needed	Employee and project lead	None
Feedback and Performance Insights	Project-based shared agreements	▪ Project agreements are key to driving feedback discussions and coaching. ▪ At key milestones or on a mutually agreed-upon schedule, the project lead and employee check in to see if they are on plan and getting what is expected from their collaboration. ▪ Employees and managers are encouraged to solicit feedback during the project check-ins. The goal is to build a trusted relationship that allows each individual to grow.	All employees	Key milestones or as needed or requested	Employee and project lead	None
	Online recognition and feedback	▪ As part of their social media platform, Services.com has implemented an online recognition and feedback tool. Employees can post their goals and aspirations, cheer on peers, or solicit private feedback.	All employees	When sought/ when offered	Employees	None

CONFIGURATION CATEGORY	PM PRACTICE	DESIGN NOTES	PARTICIPANTS	TIMING	OWNERSHIP	ASSESSMENT
Coaching and Mentoring	Career advisor	▪ Each employee will be assigned a career advisor within his or her practice area. Career advisors schedule one-on-one time with each advisee three times a year. The career advisor role is to coach, mentor, and advocate for the employee as needed.	All employees	Trimester check-ins	Assignments managed by HR Career advisors and employees drive process	None
Career and Development Planning	Competency and development plans by practice area	▪ Each practice area will maintain a set of defined competencies for its area of practice. Employees self-assess their capabilities using an online competency assessment. Career advisors review with advisees and approve competency assessment, as well as development plans.	All employees	Completed annually, updated throughout the year as needed	Employee and career advisor	Competency self-assessment against expected capabilities
	Career advisor team discussions	▪ Career advisors run a quarterly meeting with their advisees as a group to enhance collaboration and knowledge sharing. ▪ Peer feedback is encouraged as group builds trust.	All employees group by career advisor	Quarterly meetings	Career advisor	None
Talent Reviews and Insights	Global talent inventory by practice area	▪ Practice area leaders will use aggregate competency data to gain insights into the global talent mix, organizational needs, and level of capability.	Practice leaders/ executive team/HR	Annual planning/ quarterly review	Practice leaders	Talent analytics used to assess gaps
	Practice leaders conduct annual talent review process	▪ Practice leaders will conduct a talent review annually with the career advisors within their practice area. The goal of these reviews is to discuss top talent, rising stars, capability gaps, role advancement, and talent mobility strategies to support growth of the global team.	Career advisors	Annual	Practice leaders	None

CONFIGURATION CATEGORY	PM PRACTICE	DESIGN NOTES	PARTICIPANTS	TIMING	OWNERSHIP	ASSESSMENT
Total Rewards	Project manager rewards pool	▪ Project leaders will be given a small pool of reward money to allocate to the team as they see fit so they can recognize key contributions and successes.	All employees	Ad hoc	Project managers	Contribution call-out
	Capability-based compensation	▪ Career advisors will notify practice leaders when one of their advisees has advanced to the next pay band because he has increased his core capabilities. Career advisors are accountable for confirming new capability levels using the competency model and by checking in with all recent project leaders of their advisee.	All employees	Triggered by career advisor noting advancement	Practice leaders	Advancement noted/ validated against competency model
	Team-based profit sharing	▪ Profit sharing paid semiannually against team goals.	All employees with >12 months' tenure	Semiannual	Team leaders	Team metrics and targets

MY FAVORITE PM PRACTICE. The employees at Services.com loved moving away from the annual review to a project-based shared agreement. Why? Because the project agreement has a much tighter relationship to their work and their day-to-day focus. It also helps keep the dialogue open between the project leaders and team members (see figure 8.6).

Figure 8.6. Services.com shared agreement.

Shared Agreement for Project Phoenix
February 14, 2016

Project lead: *Alan*   Project resource: *Leah*

Project lead to complete: **Project employee to complete:**
Project role expectations . . .   Project experiences sought . . .
Key deliverables . . .   Capabilities to grow . . .
Project milestones/timing . . .   Success means together we . . .
Success means together we . . .

Considering the Global Organization

Managing performance at a global level warrants some serious additional thought. You must have a solid understanding of the legislative and regulatory issues, demographic trends, and labor laws from every jurisdiction in which you've got people. But all that said, I believe the most critical global consideration is to understand the cultural differences in your workforce. As Peter Drucker points out, "What managers *do* worldwide is about the same, but *how* they do it is different from culture to culture"[4] (italics mine).

If we were to take a peek at what organizations have historically done to recognize these differences, we'd see that the tactics range dramatically from barely a nod (bad) to localized approaches custom designed for each unique culture (good). Sadly, barely a nod tends to prevail. Many global organizations continue to struggle to optimize their talent management processes in the ever-expanding global market.

So what is the right approach for implementing a global workforce? Well, I'll say it again: there is no one-size-fits-all global solution. But if you agree with me that culture is the most important factor, then you'll be sure to put a respectable amount of effort into understanding those cultural differences and how they will weigh into your solution design. In other words, they are quite likely to influence your overall philosophy (and thus your design principles), so they'll require you to get aligned on how you plan to manage various global employee groups differently.

If you want to gain an appreciation for what will and won't work here, I recommend turning to the extensive research conducted by Geert Hofstede on cultures in the workforce.[5] In his research, Hofstede found five fundamental value dimensions that can be used to explain cultural diversity in the world. His "five-dimensional model" is one of the only models out there that's based on rigorous cultural research, rather than opinion—which is why I like it. The five dimensions are as follows:

1. **Power distance (PDI):** The degree to which people accept that power is distributed unevenly within a group or society.

2. **Individualism (IDV):** The degree to which taking responsibility for oneself is more valued than belonging to a group that will look after its people in exchange for loyalty.

3. **Masculinity (MAS):** The degree to which people value performance and the status that derives from it, rather than quality of life and caring for others.

4. **Uncertainty avoidance (UAI):** The degree to which people develop mechanisms to avoid uncertainty.

5. **Long-term orientation (LTO):** The degree to which people value long-term goals and have a pragmatic approach, rather than being normative and short-term oriented.

What does all this mean for designing performance systems? Well, to clarify, let's take a look at the traditional review process. The annual review is a widely accepted practice in countries like the United States and the UK. In the United States (and other countries with similar cultures), we score low on power distance and high on individualism. With those defining cultural factors, we find it easy to accept the idea that direct feedback is "the right way" to improve performance. This notion falls flat in high-power-distance countries, such as Japan and China. In fact, direct feedback in these cultures is likely to be seen as dishonorable and disrespectful. This means that we have to take a different approach that fits these cultural norms and expectations.

Another interesting dimension to consider is how your planning horizon may vary from culture to culture. When I was at Hitachi Consulting, I learned to appreciate the very real impact of working within an organization heavily influenced by Japanese leadership. One of the most notable differences was the manner in which the Japanese leaders thought about the short view and the long view. In the United States, we had a much shorter planning horizon, in contrast to our Japanese peers. This difference in focus radically influenced how each group defined what "good" looked like in both the short and long terms, as the very definition of those time frames varied radically from location to location. At times this created conflict and stress when setting targets and measuring success.

Rewarding equitably can be another tricky area as you navigate from culture to culture. The cash-is-king individual performance bonuses that we default to in countries such as the United States and the UK are not a good fit in cultures that focus on greater responsibility, larger spans of control, and wider territories as preferred rewards. Again, this showed up in my experience at Hitachi; the Japanese executives were quite surprised by our vice president's bonus model, while the US leaders were struck by their Japanese counterparts' lavish spending allowances. As they say, different strokes for different folks (or, in this case, different cultures, different expectations). In some cultures, cash rewards may even be perceived as petty. The headline? Tread carefully in this arena. If you're planning a bonus program, be sure to consider which cultures value and expect bonuses, how you should measure them if you use them, and whether team or individual incentives would work best.

Beginning to feel a bit overwhelmed? Let me reinforce a few ideas that may help keep you grounded. First, when building your design team, remember to include individuals who can help you understand these cultural differences. They can be a voice for what will work and what is likely to fall flat. Get comfortable with allowing for differences across cultures. Your goal will be to find the best balance between meeting your desire for consistency and creating great experiences for your global team. Also, before you roll out your solution, test it in different geographies and cultures—not just the solution itself, but also the supporting content, since some degree of localization is likely to be needed on that as well. In the end, keep humanity at the forefront of your design, and never forget that this is about your people, not the process!

Story #3: Tech.com

THE STARTING PLACE. Tech.com is a fast-moving, forward-thinking technology company. They hire mostly systems engineers who are young and highly skilled—in other words, hard to get in the door and even harder to keep. Tech.com is a young company in their space, but they have proved that they have the chops to leapfrog the bigger players, since they've got innovative products and better speed to market. As you might expect from an organization comprising mostly millennials and techies, they cringe at any whiff of bureaucracy.

THE DESTINATION. The Tech.com leaders are seeking a way to inspire and keep the best technical talent without bogging them down in forms, processes, and red tape. They also need to keep their teams forward-thinking and tuned in to what's going on in their market and how the technology is advancing. The company is doubling in size every twelve to eighteen months, and at that pace, training and onboarding new employees is a massive challenge.

TECH.COM'S DESIGN PRINCIPLES AND FRAME. The CEO engaged a small group of her best development leads and solution architects to help create a performance solution for their unique environment and needs. Here's what they came up with (see figure 8.7).

The Tech.com team decided on the following design principles:

The new performance management solution will . . .

1. Differentiate rewards to those who deliver great solutions, on time

2. Accelerate the growth of developer skills and capabilities

3. Eradicate any noise; what matters is what you deliver

4. Pay at market based on engineer maturity model

5. Insist on current market knowledge

Figure 8.7. Tech.com's frame.

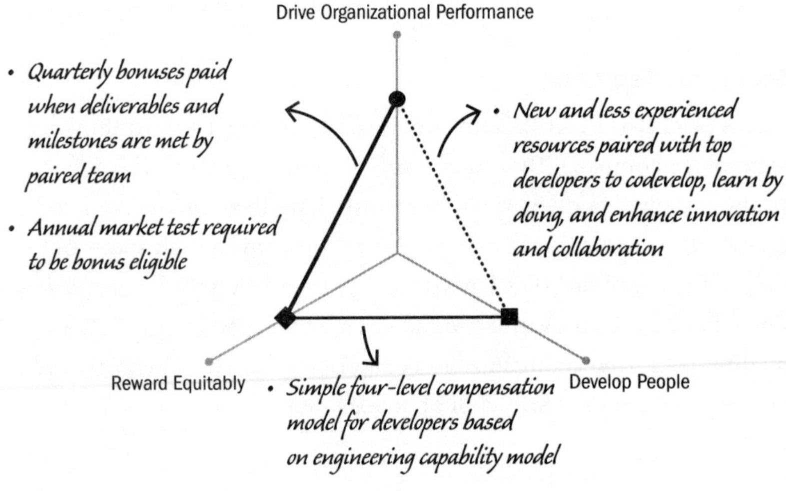

Drive Organizational Performance

- *Quarterly bonuses paid when deliverables and milestones are met by paired team*

- *Annual market test required to be bonus eligible*

- *New and less experienced resources paired with top developers to codevelop, learn by doing, and enhance innovation and collaboration*

Reward Equitably

- *Simple four-level compensation model for developers based on engineering capability model*

Develop People

TECH.COM'S CONFIGURATION. With the goal of keeping it as simple as possible, they agreed to pilot the approach shown in figure 8.8.

Figure 8.8. Configuration example: Tech.com

CONFIGURATION CATEGORY	PM PRACTICE	DESIGN NOTES	PARTICIPANTS	TIMING	OWNERSHIP	ASSESSMENT
Goals and Alignment 	Quarterly targets for development pairs and product teams	■ Each quarter the product team lead, in collaboration with his or her team, will set the development deliverables and milestones for the quarter. Milestones are set so that their achievement can be described with a simple yes or no.	All development resources	Quarterly	Product team leaders	Deliverable based— yes or no
Feedback and Performance Insights 	Employee-driven feedback	■ Development engineers own their performance and are expected to ask for feedback when desired. Quarterly deliverable targets help them assess how they are doing.	All employees	When sought	Employee	None
Coaching and Mentoring 	Pair teams for collaborative development	■ All development is done with paired teams, with less experienced developers working side by side with more experienced employees. ■ Coaching and learning is done in real time and part of everyday routine. ■ More experienced developers benefit from the new ideas and technological know-how of their junior partners. ■ Results include fewer errors, reduced time for bug fixes, and smoother product releases.	All development resources	Ongoing	Team leaders	None
Career and Development Planning 	Progression and learning planning	■ Engineers self-assess their capabilities against engineering capability model. ■ Simple development plans.	All employees	Completed annually, updated at midyear	Employee	Capabilities self-assessment

CONFIGURATION CATEGORY	PM PRACTICE	DESIGN NOTES	PARTICIPANTS	TIMING	OWNERSHIP	ASSESSMENT
Career and Development Planning (continued)	Learning encouraged and funded	■ Learning is a priority. ■ Online courses are readily available. ■ Technical certifications are tracked. Engineers can spend up to $8K a year on approved training. Other employees budget is $5K per year	All employees	Ongoing	Employee	Completion of learning is tracked and reported.
	Market and industry knowledge	■ As part of the learning strategy, every year the CEO creates a market test to drive focus to current market, industry, and technology trends. ■ Working together and using research is encouraged; what matters is that the test is completed by all developers. ■ Failing to complete the test within the set time frame disqualifies an individual from quarterly bonus until completed test is received.	All development and product management resources	Annually	Employee	Completion— Yes/No
Talent Reviews and Insights	Product lead roundup	■ Product team leaders will meet quarterly to review resource plans and move talent across teams. The development pairs will be reviewed and possibly reassigned to promote continued learning and sharing.	Product team leads	Quarterly	CEO	None
Total Rewards	Quarterly delivery bonus	■ Quarterly bonuses will be paid when deliverables and milestones are met by the paired teams. Engineers will recognize the fact that some quarters they'll make it, and some they won't. There is no shame in missing a milestone, as it is a recognized risk in the process. Seeking help and collaboration is highly encouraged across the teams.	All employees	Ad hoc	Project managers	Contribution call-out

t

MY FAVORITE PM PRACTICE. The product team leads developed a simple form that they use to support the quarterly goals process for the paired development teams. In accordance with the product development plans, paired development teams work with their product leader to agree on key development targets and deliverables. Typically, one to four goals are set and then weighted by priority, workload, or importance. At the end of the quarter, these targets (and the assigned weighting) directly correlate with how much the team receives as their quarterly bonus (see figure 8.9).

Figure 8.9. Tech.com quarterly targets.

Competing for That Tricky STEM Talent

It seems like nearly every company I've worked with is struggling to attract and retain strong technical resources, whether or not it competes in the technology space. We can chalk up the demand to the advancement of science and technology's role in nearly every industry, service, and product out there—combined with a shortage of the necessary STEM (science, technology, engineering, and mathematics) talent to support those needs. And while there's a lot of literature available on how to meet the needs and expectations of this audience, it seems worth adding a few words on this tricky employee group, specifically in regard to performance strategies.

Let's start with the employee's point of view. While acknowledging that no two people will ever want or care about exactly the same things, we can still recognize some macro themes that come up again and again that resonate with STEM-oriented personalities. First, this group cares a great deal about their skills, knowledge, and experiences. They want to be current in their field, work with the latest and greatest in technology or science, and rub elbows with the best and brightest. Second, they like to be recognized for that mastery. This recognition can come in many forms, such as awards and certifications, patents, published works, or speaking at conferences—or simply being recognized by their peers as a "rock star" in their space. They also care deeply about having the freedom to invent, build, design, explore, and play in their field. After all, how can you ever be a master if you don't have the time and space to practice your craft?

Now let's look at what the organization needs from this group. Clearly those mastery skills are important to organizations too. Yet many companies struggle to give STEM talent the tools, training, and experiences needed to stay on the cutting edge of their field of practice. The more your performance solution can focus on identifying and aligning your best technical talent to the "coolest" work, the better.

Another common tension that organizations face is wanting all that STEM brainpower aimed at the right work, rather than being distracted by other things. To address this, we need to understand where the STEM skills live in our organization, which of those skills are critical to our business strategy, where the gaps are between what we have and what we need, and how we can optimize our resources to deliver against our highest needs. And while we definitely want to put more focus on directing that talent to the best work, we also need to balance that with this group's desire for time and space to do their own thing. When you're short on critical technical talent, it's hard not to dedicate the talent that you do have 120 percent toward your priority agenda items as a company. However, you need to be a little more flexible in order to keep this very mobile group happy. Google and other forward-thinking companies have proved that letting your people use some percentage of their time on their own pet projects pays big dividends down the line.

So how should the desires and interests of both employee and employer influence your performance design? I recommend focusing on what both care about—in other words, the win-win. Here are some ideas on how to do that:

- Keep your approach simple. Why? This group tends to hate formality and bureaucracy, so do you really want to irritate them with the process? Also, this is a valuable resource, so optimizing their time is essential.

- Push as much authority and ownership as you can down the ranks. STEM folks don't like hierarchy any more than they like bureaucracy. The flatter your structure, the better. Create more opportunities that allow them to work in networked teams with control over their own resources. This also means more employee-driven and peer-based approaches. Let them be the rock star in their crowd.

- Invest in building clear technical career paths, and in creating the content necessary to enabling and communicating those paths. Share information on how these employees can build their mastery within your organization, and provide them with resources outside the walls as well.

- Build a model where you can assess the technical skills, knowledge, and capabilities that are housed within your organization. A strong technical competency/capability model will do this. It will also help to have the technical career path agenda mentioned above.

- Ensure that your talent review processes prioritize mobility. In other words, keep your STEM talent moving to increase collaboration and the sharing of knowledge, and to enhance their growth, experiences, and learnings.

- Celebrate their brilliance (often). Find ways to highlight progress, solutions, invention, things of beauty, and innovation. This may be at a team level as much as it is at the individual level. Recognition can be as simple as a toast at the Friday happy hour or as formal and high visibility as company-wide recognition such as displaying patents or other awards prominently in the office halls, or granting innovation awards internally.

- Connect your investments and their rewards to the things these employees care about: building their mastery, recognition of that mastery, and the time and freedom to play.

Story #4: Retail.com

THE STARTING PLACE. Retail.com is a large national retailer with nearly a hundred stores in the United States and Canada. While they've been in existence for more than forty years, the past decade has seen exponential growth. Employees in the stores are hourly (with the exception of managers), and the employee mix tends to be a blend of long-tenured employees, employees who stick around for one to five years (often college students), and seasonal resources who come in at peak seasons. Beyond the sales teams, there are several other employee segments in the mix, including warehouse, a call center, an online team, and the groups at headquarters who manage marketing, merchandising, supply chain, HR, and other common back-office functions. Finally, it's worth noting that the organization has a strong history of internal advancement. In fact, many people at headquarters, including several senior leaders, started on the retail floor.

THE DESTINATION. Retail.com's fundamental belief is that happy customers equal continued business growth, and that happy customers are a result of great products and friendly, helpful service. Consequently, they have a key focus on continuing to increase the service levels that their employees provide their customers. They've also seen the fight for good talent heating up as the economy has improved. Not only do they want to be the employer of choice when competing in this hotter labor market, but also they hope to find more people who will stay longer with the team. They've found that having that solid and committed base of store employees is especially critical when entering new markets. Finally, they are interested in exploring how to build a performance management approach that works for their diverse employee groups. In recent years, it has become clear that what works for the headquarters team isn't the best solution for store employees or the warehouse crews, and vice versa.

RETAIL.COM'S DESIGN PRINCIPLES AND FRAME. Retail.com put a lot of thought into their performance strategy, which they named "@ Our Best." Early on in their design process, they made a couple of key decisions. First, they were going to design for four employee segments: sales associates in stores, headquarters employees and store managers, warehouse employees, and the call center and online teams. Second, they determined that they would create a core set of design principles that supported the entire organization, and then create one or two custom design principles that would apply only to each of the four unique employee segments. The following is what it looked like for the store sales associates.

The Retail.com team decided on the following design principles (see figure 8.10):

The new performance management solution will . . .

1. Enhance our culture of customer-centricity

2. Encourage internal movement and retention of talent

3. Build and reward great managers

4. Customize our approach to the unique needs of our employee segments while maintaining a consistent core

5. Empower store managers to drive team experience

6. Reward stores for strong performance at the team level

Figure 8.10 Retail.com's frame.

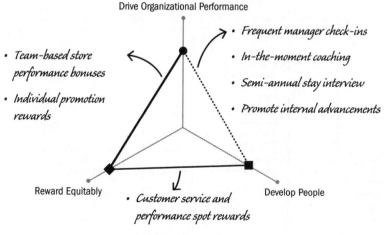

RETAIL.COM'S CONFIGURATION. Retail.com aimed to keep @ Our Best simple for the store associates. Figure 8.11 shows their configuration.

Figure 8.11. Configuration example: Retail.com.

CONFIGURATION CATEGORY	PM PRACTICE	DESIGN NOTES	PARTICIPANTS	TIMING	OWNERSHIP	ASSESSMENT
Goals and Alignment 	Sales and promotional targets	■ Store managers work with the merchandising unit to create key promotions in support of sales initiatives, product releases, and seasonal specials. ■ Sales targets are set by store for promotional windows. ■ Store targets are team based. ■ Some individual targets or sales competitions are periodically introduced.	All sales associates	Varies by sales promotion and season	Merchandising teams/ store managers	Performance against targets
Feedback and Performance Insights 	Manager check-ins	■ Emphasize developing store manager people-leadership skills and capabilities. Frequent check-ins from store managers. Managers on the floor each day. ■ Goals include catching people doing things right; finding coachable minutes; bringing team together periodically on the floor to share ideas, information, tips.	All sales associates	Ongoing	Store manager	None
	Customer feedback	■ Customer feedback is gathered in a number of ways and tracked by the store managers. ■ Positive messages are posted, with accolades, in the back room. ■ Issues or concerns are reviewed with employees as soon as they're received.	All sales associates	Ongoing	Store manager	Customer ratings of experience
Coaching and Mentoring 	Manager check-ins	■ See feedback and performance insight.	All sales associates	Ongoing	Store manager	None

CONFIGURATION CATEGORY	PM PRACTICE	DESIGN NOTES	PARTICIPANTS	TIMING	OWNERSHIP	ASSESSMENT
Coaching and Mentoring (continued)	Employee stay interview	▪ Managers meet with each store employee to gather insights on how things are going, aspirations, and areas of interest. ▪ Employees are encouraged to ask questions, explore opportunities, and seek feedback.	All sales associates	Semi-annually	Store manager	Employee profile is completed/assessment of advancement potential is added.
Career and Development Planning	Internal job postings	▪ All positions within the organization are posted on the company intranet. Store employees are encouraged to apply for positions of interest. ▪ Employees are encouraged to work with their store manager when interested in advancing, to help prepare them and help them assess readiness.	All employees	Ongoing	Employee	Self-assess against qualifications
	Employee portal stories: @ Our Best	▪ Stories of team associates are shared on the internal employee portal. ▪ Several short videos share stories of store associates who have successfully moved into other roles within Retail.com. ▪ Stories of longtime sales associates and the value they bring are also shared on the site.	All employees	Ongoing	Employee	N/A
Talent Reviews and Insights	Store manager team discussions	▪ Top performers and people ready for potential advancement are discussed at the semiannual store manager meetings. ▪ Discussion includes review of Retail.com needs across the store network and in other departments. ▪ Opportunities to advance or move talent are captured and planned at this time.	Store managers	Semi-annually	HR-facilitated discussion	Promotion/advancement list is created based on store manager nominations.

CONFIGURATION CATEGORY	PM PRACTICE	DESIGN NOTES	PARTICIPANTS	TIMING	OWNERSHIP	ASSESSMENT
Total Rewards	Tenure-based hourly rates	Sales associates' hourly rates are established by a tenure-based model with adjustments for market differentials.	All sales associates	Semi-annually	Store managers	Tenure based
	Team-based bonus for store performance	Stores are allocated a pool of bonus dollars based on their overall performance. Store manager allocates based on hours worked in period.	All sales associates	Monthly	Store managers	Hours as the variable in % of allocation
	Customer service and performance spot rewards	Store managers have a pool of spot rewards to be used to recognize great service and top performance.	All sales associates	Ad hoc	Store managers	As assessed by store manager
	Individual promotion rewards	Periodic promotional programs or events allow individuals to compete for rewards such as trips and dinner gift certificates.	All sales associates	As planned in the seasons or by event	Merchandise team/ store manager	Aligned with specific targets by promotion

MY FAVORITE PM PRACTICE. Every six months, the store managers gather for a couple of days to share best practices, celebrate top-performing stores, learn about new programs, and talk about their teams. To support the preparation for the team conversation and to make the sharing of information easy, Retail.com built a simple employee profile form (see figure 8.11). Managers complete the form every six months for each of their team members. It's extremely useful to have this information in a common format that allows sharing with other managers, and the very process of gathering the information and tuning in to each member of the store team has also proved to be of very high value. Quite simply, the nature of the exercise they call "stay interviews" reminds managers to ask those basic questions about the employees' experiences, interests, desire for advancement, and level of satisfaction—questions that help people feel valued and listened to. Having engaged their people, managers can also easily identify those on their team who might be ready to move into management or take on more responsibility in the store or in other departments within Retail.com. And frankly, it never hurts to know who's perfectly happy just staying in their sales roles.

Figure 8.11. Retail.com stay interview guide.

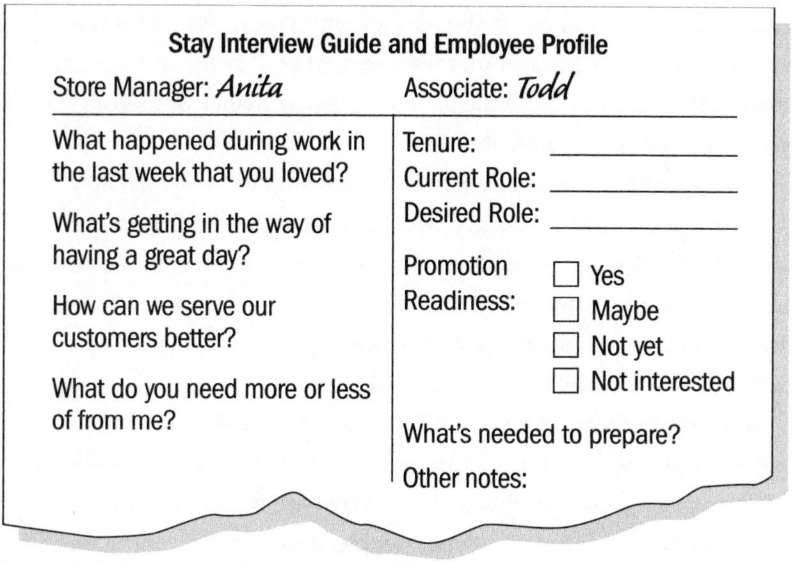

Stay Interview Guide and Employee Profile	
Store Manager: *Anita*	Associate: *Todd*
What happened during work in the last week that you loved? What's getting in the way of having a great day? How can we serve our customers better? What do you need more or less of from me?	Tenure: _____ Current Role: _____ Desired Role: _____ Promotion Readiness: ☐ Yes ☐ Maybe ☐ Not yet ☐ Not interested What's needed to prepare? Other notes:

Don't Overlook Hourly Workers

I've encountered a lot of people who think that these "modern" performance ideas don't really relate to hourly or task-oriented roles. Be careful not to fall into that line of thinking. People are people, and whatever their role in an organization, they are all likely to "show up human." They all want to be part of something, believe that what they do matters, and feel recognized for their contributions. Further, don't make the mistake of assuming that all hourly employees are alike. They run the gamut from the shop-floor worker to the administrative assistant who welcomes you to the office each morning, and their needs and expectations might be very different. That said, there *are* commonalities that are worthy of thought if you have hourly and task-oriented roles in your organization.

First, you'll often find that monetary rewards actually work well in this group, as employees in these roles are commonly paid less than their salaried coworkers. If this is the case, connect monetary rewards to near-term accomplishments. For example, monthly performance bonuses can be a great way to reward a manufacturing team, a construction crew, or groups that share similar attributes. Designing more near-term rewards will require you to get clear on measurement and create mechanisms for sharing those metrics with the team (e.g., performance or metrics boards posted in work environments).

Did you note the word *team* in that last sentence? Task-oriented departments are often managed best at the team level rather than individually. When designing your solution, find ways to push more responsibility and ownership of performance to the team as a whole. This may drive an uptick in performance, since self-managed teams have been known to create meaningful results.

It may complicate things if a union is involved, as this might limit your rewards options. In that case, turn your focus to driving organizational performance by creating greater connectivity to the value of the work, as well as the development of your people. In union environments, offering tools to help individuals build capabilities and skills can be a significant motivator, since mastering skills often aids employees in their advancement efforts.

Finally, whether you're talking about the administrative assistant or the packaging team at the end of the manufacturing line, I recommend finding ways to connect your hourly employees to your customers. It's a great motivator for them to hear directly from both internal and external customers about what is of value. It's also a powerful mechanism for creating more meaning in their work. Think about it: is the performance of that administrative assistant likely to be measured by his internal customers (i.e., the people he supports) on how many words he types per minute or for the little details he manages and the extra effort he takes to personalize his approach? Make sure that they understand what matters to those customers and that they're celebrated and rewarded for delivering on that promise. This works equally well in production environments, so don't shy away from bringing the customer's voice to those who directly influence the product or service they receive.

Write Your Own Story

I hope this chapter has helped to bring those theoretical ideas from the redesign process into clearer focus, and that the stories I've shared have inspired and energized you for the path ahead. However, I must add a word of warning before we move on to building and finally rebooting your program: as tempting as it may be to simply lift the design in one of these case studies and slap it onto your organization, resist that urge at all costs! Never forget that performance management solutions must vary from organization to organization so that they best support the various strategic needs, cultures, maturities, and business climates of each. Your solutions will, and should, look different from those of any other organization in the world—*because there is no other company exactly like yours.*

Part III

REBOOT.

*The world hates change,
yet it is the only thing
that has brought progress.*

—Charles Kettering

Let's Get Real

YOU'VE COME A LONG WAY. In Rethink, you shored up your background on the flaws of old-school performance programs, you wrapped your brain (and, I hope, your heart) around the Fundamental Shifts, and you grounded yourself in the common goals of performance management. In Redesign, your team did the hard work of designing a solution that is unique to your strategy, your culture, and your promise to your employees—with the support of your leaders and other key influencers within your organization. And now that your solution is configured, it's time to roll up your sleeves and make this design a living, breathing reality.

It's natural at this point to ask yourself how you're going to get your amazing custom performance management solution into the hands of your people in a way that ensures that they are ready to use it effectively. You'll be happy to know that answering that question—as best I can—is my goal for this final section. However, don't forget that your path from here on out may stray far from everyone else's, because your design is one of a kind. That means I can't give you as much targeted help as I did in the earlier phases, simply because I don't know what your design looks like. If I describe in detail how to build a sturdy-framed commuter bike and you've designed a unicycle, what good is that? What I can do, however, is provide a bit of guidance on how to proceed, where to focus, and how to manage many of the variables that will influence the steps typically involved in bringing any PM design into reality.

Then, in chapter 10 I'll provide some targeted help on the topic of managing change, because change—even a positive change such as an amazing new performance management solution—is hard for people. When managed poorly, it can derail even the best-laid plans and the most original and masterful designs. I'll share some ideas on helping your people come to grips with the changes in order to really connect with your new solution. And by connecting, I'm talking about acceptance, understanding, adoption, and making good use of your spanking-new approach to performance management.

Chapter 9
BUILD AND IMPLEMENT

Mobilize	*Sketch*	*Configure*	**Build**	*Implement*
Plan, invite participants, and get started	Align on your principles of design	Configure, test, and validate your solution	Build your solution, manage dependencies	Plan the change, implement, and evaluate

WHILE THE FIRST THREE PHASES of our PM Reboot process can be a wild ride, the nice thing about them is that you usually can control the process and the timeline as you see fit. But don't expect that degree of control to last into Build and Implement. These final process phases will have far more variability because of the many dependencies that are impacted by performance programs. These dependencies often include the business calendar, other talent programs and initiatives, system and tool requirements for development and implementation, and the readiness of your team to take on the shifts you're introducing. You will find that understanding and managing these dependencies is absolutely imperative in these final two phases. You're going to have to spend some time on them in addition to the creative and tactical work of designing and creating the tools and content that will support your ultimate solution. So instead of telling you exactly how to build each of your PM Practices, let me instead share my experiences in managing those many dependencies in order to help you look like an implementation superstar.

CAPTURE YOUR SOLUTION VISUALLY. A picture paints a thousand words, they say, and you've devoted a lot more than a thousand words to discussing the design process. So with the design work complete, it's time to make sure you've captured your design in a way that is comprehensive and easy to understand and share by creating a picture of it. Not only is a visual image an important tool for guiding your work during the Build and Implement phases, but also it's immensely valuable as a way to make sure your stakeholders have a shared understanding of how all the pieces (in this case, your PM Practices) come together. When done well, a great visual summary will carry you from the early validation of your solution design right through training and onboarding. I provide suggestions and examples for how to create your visual at **www.thePMReboot.com.**

MANAGE YOUR SOLUTION DEPENDENCIES. The three dependencies that are most likely to influence you in the Build and Implement phase are other talent management processes and programs, systems and tools requirements, and processes that you don't own, such as strategic planning. It's critical that you dedicate sufficient time and energy to understanding, planning, and staying on top of these dependencies.

DEVOTE TIME TO TALENT MANAGEMENT INTEGRATION. While I don't know what your solution looks like, I can bet that you have dependencies on other areas of talent management. It's rare that you wouldn't. Depending on the structure of your HR/people/TM team, you may own those other areas, or you may not. Either way, when planning your build and implementation, you have to understand the level of integration that your solution will require with the other talent management disciplines. Some expectations for integration may be crystal clear, while others may require a bit more planning and focus.

Let's explore this topic using an example from one of my clients. As shown on our flip chart, this client placed a high priority on providing visibility into global talent capabilities; in fact, it was one of their top design principles (see figure 9.1). It looks straightforward on the surface, but when you dig into the principle, you realize that it has quite a few gnarly tentacles that extend into other branches of talent management. In other words, there's no way to make this part of the design a reality without changing the way things are done in those other areas.

Figure 9.1. Client example.

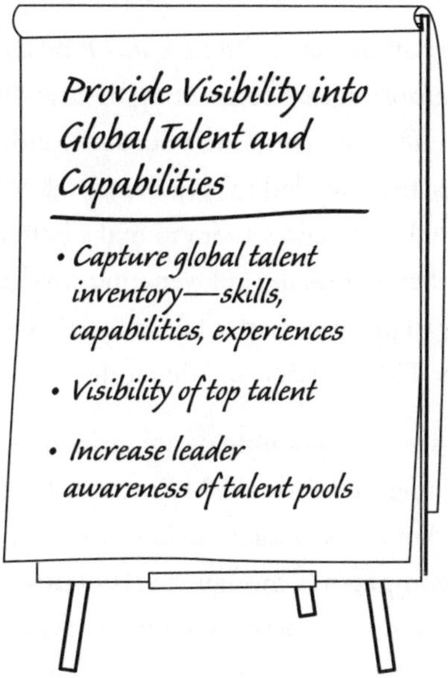

To expose these connections, let's look at the PM Practices that were selected to deliver on this design principle:

- In support of *developing people,* they selected a PM Practice of asking employees to complete self-assessments of their capabilities against a role-based competencies model. Doing so helps employees understand their areas of strength and what development they'll need in order to improve in their current roles and prepare for their future ones. In aggregate, this collected data provides an organizational view of their talent portfolio. However, to deliver this design element, they need clear job frameworks and an agreed-upon method by which people can assess their skills and capabilities. This is something they'd look to the talent management team to provide.

- Leaning a bit more toward the *reward equitably* side (though with a toe still in *develop people* territory), they picked a PM Practice of creating a high-potential (HIPO) program that rewards strong players with stretch assignments. So now their design has a dependency on the HIPO program as well as a reliable talent mobility process and supporting protocols.

- Finally, let's turn our attention to *drive organizational performance.* They made the assumption that connecting the right people to the right roles will enhance execution. In order to enhance those people connections, they needed to give their leaders improved visibility into their talent to allow them to make better and timelier decisions. So now they're looking at leveraging strong talent analytics capability to produce better talent insights for their leaders. Yet another TM interface and dependency.

In short, to make this seemingly simple design principle a reality, the client selected and configured several PM Practices that are highly integrated with several other areas of talent management, including role frameworks and related competency models, a HIPO program, talent mobility, and talent analytics. Like them, you need to build out your future solution while carefully noting and working through all the areas that the solution touches. When all is said and done, it is likely that these dependencies will impact the staging of your solution and your implementation timing. Be ready to manage these dependencies, take on what you can when you can, plan for future enhancements as capabilities become available, and build your plan with a holistic and realistic view.

MANAGE YOUR SYSTEM DEPENDENCIES AND OWN YOUR TECH-NOLOGY STRATEGY. I haven't spent much time speaking to the technology side of all this, largely because I want you to build the solution that's right for you without being unduly influenced by the technology options. Too often I've come across teams that are banking on technology alone to cure all their performance management woes. Sure, new tools may smooth out a few of the bumps and might even make oversight and status tracking easier, but pushing a poorly designed solution faster and more efficiently around your organization doesn't make a whole lot of sense. The power of workflow and automated templates will not get you better results or increase the engagement of your team.

If you take nothing else away from this book regarding technology tools and systems, let it be this: *design first, technology second.* You may want to understand some of the system options along the way, and that's fine, but please don't get so mesmerized by the bells and whistles that software vendors are so great at selling that you lose your design in the process. You will need to decide if and where you will use technology to enable your solution. This could be as simple as a shared drive to house individual commitments or as comprehensive as a full-fledged talent management system. If your team doesn't have the budget for a new technology-enabled solution, fret not. A variety of options and tools are available today that range from very traditional models to more modern social media platforms.

An important note here is that technology often can become a dominant driver of the timeline. If you have a high degree of dependency on the information technology (IT) team for your solution, be sure to involve them every step of the way, and be prepared to give, as well as take, when it comes to integrating your needs into the IT master plan. Here are a few tips:

- If the IT needs are slowing you down, assess whether you can start out low-tech, then build capability over time as the technology becomes available to you.

- If you are working with IT to enable your solution, build a strong partnership and be very clear on your requirements. *Be certain that it's the solution design driving your end result, not your technology defaults or constraints.*

If your technology strategy takes you out into the market to look for a new system, you'll find that the technology for performance management and talent solutions continues to be in a state of transition. Talent management tech providers are racing to provide their customers a fully integrated talent management suite, often acquiring smaller providers to fill in gaps and enhance functionality. At the same time, we're seeing more point solutions and social platform tools entering the market and providing a wider range of options to explore. Be aware that many of the long-standing performance management tools are anchored in the traditional methods of performance management. Granted, they've enhanced their offerings with workflow, tracking, and reporting tools, and have also integrated with learning, development, and compensation platforms. However, they've been slow to move away from the traditional model and the faulty assumptions that come with it. We are also seeing increasing numbers of new entrants into the performance management tech arena, primarily those that use social platforms to introduce new approaches to setting goals, enabling peer recognition, and more.

Take a broad look at the market and choose wisely. When you can, I recommend piloting the tools prior to signing up for any long-term contracts. Many of the social tools make testing their wares easy to do, and I've found that the experience can be quite enlightening, since it allows you to find out what you like and don't like about how they operate. While these social tools can seem trendy and cool, you may find that they don't fit the work style or culture of your organization.

Another dimension of technology to consider during your detail design is the capturing of performance data through other technologies. For example, call center systems can now provide visibility into how people share knowledge and support each other, in addition to standard productivity data. Other examples include project management systems, customer relationship management (CRM), and knowledge management systems for professional services. Designing your solution to incorporate these insights can be helpful as long as you're consistent with your principles of design and the measurement technique is integrated into the way people work and not a stand-alone process requiring a separate effort.

While selecting the right technology solution can seem daunting at times, the good news is that many of these advances in technology are bringing more options and capabilities to users. Just don't get sold on features you don't need. Design first, do your homework, and select your technology wisely.

MANAGE YOUR DEPENDENCIES EXTERNAL TO THE SOLUTION. In addition to the dependencies within both your solution and the talent arena, it is common that elements of your new solution will have relationships with processes outside of performance management, such as strategic planning. Capture any of these dependencies, and note the next steps required to work through your dependency. At times you may need to ask others to change their approach to meet your needs. This means that you will need to work collaboratively with the owners of these external dependencies to define how you'll get from where you are today to where you want to go in the future.

Oversee the Build-Out and Plan the Rollout

Let's not underestimate how much hard work needs to be done during Build and Implement to create the content, shore up your plan, and get this solution into the hands of your people. While managing the dependencies may take considerable political skills, the rollout will require nothing less than creativity, salesmanship, elbow grease, and an ample supply of patience. This is where the nuts-and-bolts work is done and hundreds of detailed decisions are made. It's also where your dreams of a new performance experience finally come true.

CREATE YOUR BUILD PLAN. The build plan is the master planning document that defines the deliverables that need to be built to support your solution. The build plan should define the key requirements of the items to be designed and should capture design notes, assign resources, and estimate the time required to get it all done. If it requires outside investments, you may also want to include the estimated cost to build. To create your build plan, go back through your configuration content, as well as any visual or summarized capture of your solution, and inventory what needs to be designed and built out, including templates, tools, agendas, and supporting content.

PLAN YOUR CHANGE. You certainly don't want to put all this effort into your design and then have it rejected by your team because you didn't ready them for this change. In fact, this is such an important topic that I devote all of chapter 10 to it.

REASSESS AND EVOLVE YOUR ROLLOUT STRATEGY AND TIMELINE. Now that your solution is designed and you have a clear view of your dependencies (talent management, systems, and external), it's the perfect time to go back and reassess that journey plan we talked about back in Mobilize. Reconsider your rollout strategy and timeline. Does it still make sense to roll out the changes for the new solution the way you originally planned, or are there elements in the design that require you to make some changes? There's no shame in reworking at this point—in fact, the opposite is true. Remember, you can play with how you will cascade your solution across the organization, as well as how you might phase the solution itself. You've invested a lot of time and effort in building a great solution, so be thoughtful about how you will introduce it to the full organization.

CREATE SUPPORTING CONTENT. Throughout this journey, you'll have created several artifacts that define and bring your solution to life, such as your design principles, configuration summary, and the visual discussed above. These items can often be converted into content that will help you ready people for the planned changes and ease their transition to the "new normal." Perhaps they become learning aids, training materials, or online tools. It's likely that you'll identify other content that needs to be created specifically to aid in implementation. When building your list, consider items such as simple process flows, RACI (roles and responsibility) charts, a calendar of events, expectation guides, FAQ (frequently asked questions), examples, learning tools, descriptions of templates or tools, and so on.

DEFINE YOUR SUSTAINABILITY MODEL. Your new performance management solution is a living process, which means that it should continue to evolve with the changing needs of your people and your organization, as well as with changes in the external environment. You also may want to adjust things as you gain experience with the new approach and learn what's working well and what isn't. To recognize this, articulate your sustainment plan by answering these questions:

- Who is the owner of the solution/process?

- How often will you review and update the solution?

- How will you capture feedback and assess needs for refinements and changes?

- How will you govern the proposed changes? Who will participate in the governance process?

Bravo! You've just completed the five phases of the PM Reboot process. On first read, these past five chapters dedicated to the PM Reboot process may have taken you days or even weeks to absorb. (See the process image in figure 9.2 to get a quick recap of the steps you've completed.) Of course, as an author, I love the thought of you clinging to every word while imagining yourself bravely leading your enthusiastic cohorts to the performance management promised land. But I know it's equally likely that you just spent a half-hour or so flipping through the book over a burrito and a soda at lunch just to get the general idea. If so, I can honestly say that it doesn't hurt my feelings in the least. I realize that was some very heavy lifting, so hats off if you were able to fully commit to the material the first time around. If you weren't up for investing that level of time and energy just yet, that's OK, too. I'm happy to acknowledge that not everyone who picks up this book is ready to dive headfirst into the process. I present these process chapters with the idea that you will return to them again and again when the time is right. Whether that's next week or two years from now, this step-by-step guide, as well as the Toolbox and web-based materials that accompany it, will be here when you need them.

Figure 9.2. The PM Reboot process recap.

Mobilize	*Sketch*	*Configure*	*Build*	*Implement*
Plan, invite participants, and get started	Align on your principles of design	Configure, test, and validate your solution	Build your solution, manage dependencies	Plan the change, implement, and evaluate

Mobilize
- Lead your leaders
- Plan journey
- Invite the right people to the conversation

Sketch
- Know your starting place
- Understand your destination
- Align on your design principles
- Sketch your frame

Crowdsource your design principles

Configure
- Configure your solution
  - Brainstorm
  - Select
  - Confirm
  - Configure
- Test your configuration

Build / Implement
- Prepare for Build and implementation
  - Capture your solution visually
  - Manage dependencies (internal TM, & external)
  - Define your systems and technology strategy
  - Create your build plan
  - Plan your change
  - Reassess and evolve your timeline
  - Create supporting content
  - Define your sustainability model

Chapter 10
MAKING IT STICK

WE ALL KNOW OF, OR PERHAPS have even been part of, teams that
have devoted huge efforts and resources to revamping a process, only
to have it fail miserably. People don't get onboard. Resources dry up.
Resistance builds. Leaders abandon ship, claiming they weren't really
keen on it to begin with. Confusion or disenchantment arises—and
in the end, the potential value is never realized.

Don't let the new performance management solution you worked
so hard to build suffer this cruel fate. As you lead the charge toward
improved performance management in your organization, you'll need
a strategy to stay there once you arrive. A thoughtful approach to
managing the change is your best investment to ensure that your hard
work of creating a custom, modern performance management solution
for your organization won't be for naught.

With that in mind, throughout this chapter I'll help you consider how
to cement the buy-in, adoption, and sustainability of your new solution.
The guidance provided is by no means a comprehensive change management program; instead, I highlight important considerations to drive
adoption and share helpful tips for managing the often-unavoidable
resistance you're likely to face. I have much more that I want to share
related to managing the human side of this shift, but it is simply too
much to provide within these pages. (The next book, perhaps?) As a
happy compromise, I have included additional change content and
tools at our website **www.ThePMReboot.com**. In the end, I hope this
chapter, the "Support and Buy-in Checkpoint" tips in the Redesign, and
the additional website resources can supply you with a strong framework and meaningful insights that will ensure that your new approach

to performance management is well received, gains support quickly, and has real staying power within your organization.

Your New Job One: Leading the Change

Don't even think about using a one-and-done email from the CEO to announce to your organization the exciting news that you're replacing the old performance management system. There is no communication so well crafted that it will get everyone onboard and excited after it's a done deal. No slick video message, no dog-and-pony show, no rah-rah meeting with cake, pizza, or champagne can possibly replace the value of simply getting people involved.

Why not? you ask. Can't a well-managed staff just do as they're told without all the touchy-feely stuff? No, they can't. That's just not how it works.

The urge to get moving before everyone's truly onboard is understandable, but there's considerable upside to slowing down a bit. When change management is done well, people will feel engaged in the process and work collectively toward a common objective—in this case, your new performance management solution. How engaged, you ask? Well, I'll tell you: effective change management increases the success rate of organizational change as much as 96 percent.[1] Furthermore, research has shown that projects with excellent change management effectiveness are six times more likely to meet or exceed project objectives.[2] Building a great solution and then failing to manage the change effectively is like building a high-performance racing bike and leaving the wheels off.

When you're fired up about making a change (especially with something as earthshaking as a new performance management program), it can be hard to tolerate those who aren't tuned in, don't get it, or worse yet, are resistant and unwilling to fully commit to it. When you find yourself in that situation, take a deep breath and look at how far you've come. Remember that your own journey started some time ago, and not everyone has been traveling with you. Your job now is to meet the rest of your team where they are (no matter how frustrating it can be at times) and invest the time and effort in bringing them forward. Engaging your organization in your new program means that your employees need to know what is happening and why, understand how it will impact them, and be equipped to be successful after the change is made. This is not the place to cut corners, because a great new solution is only truly great if people understand its purpose, see its value, are equipped to use it, and feel rewarded for doing so.

Make the Case

The best foundation for building meaningful support and ensuring buy-in of your future solution is a strong case for the change. This means creating a compelling story that tells your team why *now* is the time for a new approach to performance management and inspires them to dream of a better way, too.

The funny thing about change is that it's hard even when we know it's for the best. Why is it that people resist change, even when it's clearly constructive and necessary? Neuroscience tells us that the answer may lie in the way our brains work. Change creates stress, and stress triggers our fight-or-flight hormones. This means that while you may feel like you are making logical decisions, your emotions are actually exerting a tremendous amount of control over what you do and say. In their book *Switch,* Chip and Dan Heath make this phenomenon plain to us nonscientists by way of the simple analogy of a rider and an elephant.[3] The rider is our rational side, diligently processing away on the facts. Our emotional side is the elephant. The rider provides direction and analysis, but the elephant ultimately must supply the impetus to get things done. When it comes to a change, you can explain all you want to the rider, but if the elephant decides it's going in another direction—well, it's pretty clear who's going to win that battle. To move in a new direction, the Heath brothers say that we need to persuade both the rider *and* the elephant.

A great case for change appeals to both the rider and the elephant by communicating both the actual *and* emotional bottom line of your new solution. It needs to paint the vision of the future, share solution highlights, lay out the implementation plan, and summarize the expected outcomes, benefits, and costs. You want it to tell a great story while at the same time being short, punchy, visual, entertaining, and, above all, memorable. Honestly, truly nailing it is a tall order. Impossible? No. But it takes some work to get right.

You've been building this story since the early days of your journey. Your mission now is to review what you've learned, look at everything you've envisioned for your new solution, pick the best bits, and package that information so that it appeals to the hearts and minds of your audience. You should already have the support of key influencers and decision makers, but this story is for the rest of the folks. You need it to resonate with all of them, engaging those who are new to the story and solidifying the resolve of those who are already with you.

It might be best to start with the business side of your case by asking what the old way has cost the organization in real dollars and cents. If you haven't done it already, gauge the amount of time and resources being spent on your current approach, and then show the opportunity cost of not making a change. Few organizations have taken a hard look at the resources being consumed for so little benefit. Recent analysis conducted by CEB found that the average manager spends more than 200 hours a year on activities related to performance reviews.[4] If we apply that value to a hypothetical situation, we can easily illustrate the high cost of traditional performance management like this:

> *We have four thousand employees, including five hundred managers who each spend an average of two hundred hours a year planning for and conducting annual performance reviews. That's one hundred thousand hours a year for managers. Our employees each spend about twenty hours a year planning for and participating in their annual performance reviews. That's another seventy thousand hours. Together, that's one hundred seventy thousand work hours. At an average hourly rate of $50, that's $8.5 million a year. Are we getting good return on that investment? What else could we accomplish in one hundred and seventy thousand work hours per year?*

Or maybe your conclusions focus on your case for increasing the strategic value of HR, and your story goes something like this:

> *I asked HR to give me a sense of how much time they spent each year related to our current performance process. They said about 50 percent of the time. Shocking. Fifty percent? I asked why. They said it's largely because of the complexity of our process, which increases the time to prepare the organization and to address the many questions that arise. Then there's chasing down those who are out of compliance— missing reviews, weak assessments, etc. Lastly, they get involved in a lot of employee issues that result from the reviews. How can HR play a strategic role if they're spending all their time just overseeing the processes?*

Once you've locked the case on the business side, turn your attention to the emotional side of your performance management history. When you're speaking to the emotional elephant, it is always best to show rather than tell. John Kotter, considered to be the father of change management, tells us that "showing others the need for change with a compelling object that they can actually see, touch, and feel" is the best way to get people on board.[5] This is why advertisers use images and stories to grab our attention, and why high school driving teachers show videos of gruesome car crashes to shock their teenage students.

Selling your plan is no different. Consider what you might "show" people to engage the elephant. Maybe it's quotes from your focus groups, video clips of your people sharing their thoughts on your current approach, or a huge pile of paper that represents one year's annual reviews. Think about the focus groups, interviews, and internal and external benchmarking you did early on. Then tell the story in as compelling a manner as possible. Emphasize the human side of the equation, and connect your case for change to the values and the cultural elements that hold meaning within your organization.

If your messaging sinks in and they say, "Oh, you're right. We do need to change this," then it's time to start talking about your planned destination. Borrowing another idea from *Switch* authors Chip and Dan Heath, think about it as if you're sending them a postcard from some beautiful destination that says, "Meet me here! It's going to be great."[6] You don't need to go into detail; just share the big ideas about what your solution will bring to the organization. Your goal is to pull them into your vision of the future, and then give them enough of a plan to know what to expect and when. Keep it high level, including just enough to capture their attention—and their imaginations.

So what does this look like when you're finished? That's up to you. It could be a nicely designed walking deck, a set of short videos, a social media campaign, or some combination thereof. Again, there is no right answer; design the mode and methods of communication with your organization in mind. I'd simply encourage you to be creative, consider who your audience is, meet them where they are, and seek to create a burning platform (one from which people realize that there really is no way to go but forward) by telling your story. Channel your own passion and excitement; then climb into the pulpit and become an evangelist for change.

Plan the Change

You've designed your solution and grasped the realities related to its implementation, but all that means nothing without a great change plan. And to be truly great, your plan needs to be anchored in an understanding of how big the change is and the nature of the changes that people will experience. We also need to know who's going to be experiencing those changes and the potential impacts on them. In other words, how much will this process upset the apple carts of the people in your organization? And how many apples does this mean we're going to lose?

The amount of effort you should expect to devote to managing the change (talking to people and getting them onboard, up to speed, trained, excited, and equipped) is directly related to the size of the change. Will the changes you want to make be relatively easy to implement? Or is this going to be a tectonic shift, requiring you to pretty much blow up your existing approach, start from scratch, and perhaps rock the organization to the core of its corporate culture?

To help you identify the type of change you are looking at for your organization, you should consider the impacts, risks, and change saturation. There's a lot that can be said about each of these areas—and Beth Montag-Schmaltz, my business partner, cofounder of PeopleFirm, and change management guru, would likely argue that each one of these could warrant its own chapter (or book, for that matter). Who knows, maybe Beth will write that book someday. For our purposes, I'll touch briefly on each of these considerations.

Identify major impacts

It may seem obvious, but one of the first things you as a leader should do is take the time to identify the impacts that this change is going to have on your organization. In our business, we call this the *impact assessment.* A good impact assessment starts with getting clear on the who, as in "Who is being impacted?" We create logical groupings of the impacted people based on the nature of the changes being experienced, identifying collections of people who are starting at the same place and experiencing the change similarly. Your groups may break down into collections such as employees in general; people managers; HR business partners; executive leaders, etc. Bear in mind that considering the "who" requires you to go back to your design and reflect on those groups you identified during configuration. Did you create special programs for your high potentials? If the answer is yes, then those HIPOs probably represent their own stakeholder group, since the nature of the changes they experience will be different from what others experience.

As you go through this process, you'll begin to recognize the implications for these stakeholder groups, and the appropriate steps to best support each of them through the change process will become clear. Some areas are commonly overlooked or underestimated during impact assessments. Here are a few:

- *Role changes.* Will your new solution change the expectations for any of the roles in your organization? If you've moved away from a traditional program, I'm betting it will. For example, HR may now be out of the oversight game, and will instead need to shift focus to building content and capturing best practices to be shared back out to the organization.

- *Manager expectations.* Your people managers might have been rewarded in the past for simply getting reviews in on time, but success in their roles now might be based on how much time they spend with their teams and how effective their people say they are at helping them achieve their career goals. That's a significant change. Remember to communicate those expectation changes to others; it's helpful when everyone understands that what "good" looked like in the past may look a lot different today.

- *Skill gaps.* Undoubtedly, new skills will need to be developed in order to make your changes sustainable. The most common of these is going to be the need to retrain your managers so that they can support a more conversational, employee-driven method of developing people. You can't just expect your managers to do this well, especially those who were promoted for their technical expertise rather than their people skills. Flag where new skills are needed; then build time and effort into your change plan to adequately address these needs.

- *Employee empowerment.* While you'd expect most people to say that they'd like to be masters of their own career destiny, in reality many people are just not comfortable with this level of accountability. We've been raised to defer this responsibility to our parents, teachers, or supervisors. Getting comfortable with the idea of asking for feedback can be tough for some. This is an excellent example of a change for the better that might still get a fair amount of resistance from the people you'd least expect: the employees themselves.

Our cultural instinct is to find a place to hold us, a spot where we are safe from the responsibility/obligation/opportunity to choose. Because if we choose, then we are responsible, aren't we?
—SETH GODIN, "A BIRD IN SEARCH OF A CAGE"[7]

How do you get a handle on all these impacts? Start by simply talking to people. Work with your design team, since they know the solution best, and then ask managers, business leads, process leads, and anyone else who might provide insight into who and what will be impacted by the change. Validate your assumptions. And then be ready to adjust your plan when you start rolling out your solution, because there may be impacts you hadn't anticipated.

Assess risk

Next, take a look at the probable level of complexity of your rollout to determine how much risk you're taking on. Complexity may be driven by the number of groups you identified during your impact assessment or by the geographical and cultural differences you have to manage across those groups. It may come in the form of dependencies on things like new technology, or connecting the solution rollout to a larger effort, such as a cultural transformation or the integration of a new acquisition.

When assessing risk, you also need to consider which groups on your stakeholders list might present a higher risk either to the success of the program itself or to such things as your brand or customer experience. For example, which groups have direct customer-facing roles? You'll want to be sure that these groups are well managed so that you can reduce the risk of any ill will bleeding into your customer experience. Also consider the groups that could take the project down if they are not all-in on the plan. (How awful would it be if your own HR team torpedoed your efforts?) These high-risk teams and individuals will need the greatest care and handling. And if you've got a team that's both heavily impacted and high-risk? Those people are your first priority.

Consider change saturation

We established earlier that we're just plain wired to resist change. So what happens when you force your employees to go through too many changes at once? Bad stuff: increased employee turnover, higher likelihood of project failures, productivity losses, dissatisfaction, disengagement, and higher levels of absenteeism. Change practitioners call this *change fatigue,* and trust me, you don't want to deal with it as you're rolling out your new performance management solution. Obviously, the ideal way to avoid change saturation is to time your implementation so that no group is in the midst of too many other changes at the same time. Of course, this might not be entirely realistic in today's fast-paced business environment, but you can put some effort into coordinating with other implementation managers to avoid overloading groups of people with too much at any one time.

Create Your Change Plan

Now is the time to sit down and write up your change plan, capturing the change management activities you will be completing in order to give your new performance management solution real staying power.

This is where you decide what you plan to do to help your employees with the transition to your new performance management solution. A great change plan will consider the who (those stakeholder groups you identified earlier), the what (the nature of the change activity, such as planned communications or learning events), and the when (the right time to reach each group with this content or engagement).

(🔧) GUIDE TO CREATING YOUR CHANGE PLAN

To help you get started, check out the step-by-step facilitation guide to building your change plan in the Toolbox.

Gather Your Change Champions

Consider building a coalition of advocates that will support this effort throughout the journey. Change champions, change advocates, change support network—regardless of what you call them, they'll play a critical role in the success of your transition to a new performance management solution. You'll want to make sure that someone from each major area (department, geography, group, etc.) is represented. The role of this hand-picked group is to be educated on why the change is happening, what the new way will look like, and what the process is to get there. Their mission is to support the overall readiness of the employees and reinforce the key messages and information that you provide. Good change champions help people navigate the change and keep them pointed in the right direction. They can provide support during and after the rollout of the new solution, ensuring that people feel successful with the new ways and that they remain committed for the long term. You can also look to them to serve as two-way conduits for information, not only helping you share information with their constituencies but also providing you feedback and insights on how things are tracking.

Perhaps the most important role that change champions play is to generate enthusiasm among the masses. You simply cannot underestimate the impact that a fellow team member (someone your employees know and trust) can have in encouraging people to get onboard. These emissaries of change have strong relationships with the folks in the trenches, so their word that it's going to be great in the long run is going to resonate more powerfully than yours, no matter how elegantly you phrase your communications.

Expect Resistance

You need to expect that your new ideas and approach will encounter resistance. In fact, you should be shocked if they don't. Resistance will show up in a variety of ways and for a bunch of reasons. The roots of resistance are fairly predictable in any change effort and commonly include *fear of loss, uncertainty, surprise, change fatigue, fear of incompetence,* and *fear of increased workload.*[8] When you're assessing change impacts and the nature of resistance you might encounter, it is helpful to evaluate how stepping away from Fatal Flaws and toward the

Fundamental Shifts will trigger reactions or influence behaviors across your stakeholder groups. Here are a few examples to jumpstart your own analysis of the resistance you need to plan for:

- *Fear of loss.* The groups most commonly at risk for fear of loss resistance include your leaders, managers, and potentially members of your HR team. But what do they fear they'll be losing? Most often it's a sense of power or control. Managers may believe that to shift to an employee-powered process reduces their power within the organization. Leaders may feel that abandoning ratings and forced distributions reduces their ability to control outcomes and people decisions. HR members may think moving to a solution that varies across the organization by employee segments or groups creates chaos and reduces their ability to control consistency in the experience, quality, and outcomes.

  I recommend attacking this form of resistance head-on. Get it out in the open and talk it through with those concerned. Bring others who can share their experiences and stories into the conversation to reduce anxiety and inspire more buy-in.

- *Uncertainty.* This is a big resistance risk for designs that stray dramatically from tradition. People who have spent the entirety of their careers in top-down, manager-driven performance processes are likely to be more skeptical than most about the ideas put forward in the Fundamental Shifts. An uncertainty concern frequently raised is, "Does this new model mean we're throwing out accountability?" This concern was at the heart of an experience I had just a few weeks ago when giving a presentation to a team of executive leaders for one of our clients. The CEO's only comment about the shifts and my examples was, "We don't want any of that touchy-feely stuff."

  This prime example of resistance rearing its ugly head stemmed from his uncertainty about stepping away from what he knows and trying ideas that he's never seen in action. When you encounter these doubting Thomases, I find it helps to call on research, data, examples, and stories to help people build confidence. Piloting can also be used to a huge advantage—show them how it will work in a contained environment before you ask them to go all-in.

- *Fear of incompetence.* The apprehension that comes with questioning one's own ability to adapt to change can drive some of the greatest resistance. Even worse, it tends to show up in passive ways, making it harder to recognize. People are just plain scared of looking stupid, not getting it, or failing in this new normal. This is especially true when the pride we derive at work from our knowledge and skill is on the line. When shifting away from a generic performance management model to something more organic and holistic, you might find that HR business partners who have invested a great deal of time in designing, training others, and overseeing your old process may doubt their ability to guide people through your new process. Managers may feel woefully unprepared to discuss careers or unaccustomed to new levels of transparency and openness. It's worth identifying these risks early on and designing targeted interventions to build the confidence of those who feel exposed or at risk.

- *Fear of increased workload.* Employees and managers alike may experience this form of resistance. This perspective may be driven by the thought of scrapping annual or semiannual reviews in favor of ongoing conversations. It can also be a by-product of managers realizing that they need to take more accountability for outcomes and that they can no longer rely on HR recommendations, policies, or guidelines for easy answers. The best way to mitigate this risk is to keep your approach simple and easy to use and to provide all those involved with the necessary training to ensure that they can quickly become effective at applying the new processes, tools, and systems you've incorporated into your configuration. Shortening the learning curve can help win you early support and increase the speed of adoption.

And the list goes on. The takeaway here is that all of these responses are natural, and they represent the spectrum of emotions that are felt (even if they aren't always expressed) when change occurs. Your job is to predict them where you can, prepare to respond, be empathetic when they arise, and invest the time and energy in readying your team to embrace (or maybe even love) your new program.

Of course, knowing why resistance is to be expected doesn't entitle you to write off legitimate feedback when it's offered. That is *not* what I'm advocating here. After all, some resistance may come from folks who see legitimate weaknesses in your new approach and whose insight will ultimately produce a better result. Those are the people you want to engage early in the design process so that their voices can be heard. In short, listen to the resistance. Try to identify the underlying root of it: is it a passing concern about the upcoming changes and how they will impact the individual, or is it offered in the spirit of helping the process? Some resistance may present valuable feedback you should be internalizing, while other resistance (probably the majority) is just going to be something you have to work through with your people, who, you'll recall, are *not* machines. As the champion of the effort, you have to figure out how to get everyone there eventually. You can do this only by being thoughtful about how you manage the change and by coaxing both the rider and the elephant to make the journey with you.

Defend against the Naysayers

One busy Friday, I met with a West Coast client in the morning and then returned to my office to take a call from one of my East Coast clients in the afternoon. In the span of a few scant hours, both of my clients used exactly the same phrase to describe their current performance management programs: "Our performance management program is fine."

All weekend that phrase was stuck in my brain like an annoying popcorn hull wedged between my teeth. I pondered what those words meant to each of them and what ugly truths might lurk beneath an innocuous word like *fine*. I think that phrase spoke loudly to me because I'd heard it so many times before.

So what do people mean when they tell me that their performance program is *fine*? Perhaps it's this:

F	**FEAR.** I don't think we have the courage to take up the agenda in my organization.
	FATIGUE. We have been tweaking our process for years. After years of debate, we finally agreed on rating scales. Why change now?
I	**IMAGINATION.** We seem unable to imagine something better—we don't love it, but what else could we do? It's better to stick with what we know.
	INCONCEIVABLE. How can you assess performance without ratings? It's inconceivable without a consistent rating process.
N	**NOT MY PROBLEM.** We've built the process and tool; it's not our fault if our managers aren't good at talking to their people.
	NEVER FLY. I have no idea how to sell this to our leadership.
E	**EVERYONE ELSE DOES IT THIS WAY.** We are simply not going to be "bleeding edge" here.

In addition, the low expectations expressed in the phrase "Our performance management is fine" are indicative of how much we've lost sight of our people. We seem perfectly happy to settle for "fine" on their behalf. But if our intentions for investing in performance management are to connect our teams to our strategies and goals, to recognize outstanding contributions, and to enhance the development of each individual's capabilities, how can we possibly continue to tolerate "fine"?

When I have a debate with someone who is defending the traditional performance management approach or with someone who is fearful of making changes to such a deeply rooted process (and trust me, I have many such debates), I always hear the same counterarguments. So much so, in fact, that it's worthwhile to prepare you to answer those same objections in your own organization. See if you recognize any of these common objections.

"My boss will never buy it."

As I've discussed, it is wise to pay special attention to "the boss." Engage, educate, and bring him or her with you. Of course, you can't expect this to happen overnight, especially if the boss in question leans more toward the traditionalist mind-set. Meet leaders where they are, build a plan, pace your progress, and maintain your resolve. Find out what they really care about and connect your case to that theme. You need their elephant with you, but understand that most leaders prefer to feel as though they're always operating in the rider's world. You may have to be diplomatic and creative with your strategy to appeal to both aspects of their decision-making tandem.

"We can't trust our managers."

Other than getting leaders on board, this is the second-biggest concern I hear from people, and it's a legitimate one. Since we're considering implementing a design that relies heavily on good, or preferably *great*, managers, this problem often stops teams in their tracks. It's not a simple issue, either. It's cluttered with questions of structure, role definition, and manager expectations. Many organizations suffer from being overmanaged and under-led. This happens because we often promote managers for technical or functional expertise and not for their people or managerial skills. We also have the industrial age to thank for a legacy of too many layers of oversight, and we're only just beginning to break down those structures. Finally, most organizations have historically underinvested in building great leaders, especially in the lean years we've recently experienced. In short, all these trends add up to making the manager question a complicated and messy one, and a valid source of concern.

If this worry resonates with you, I'd encourage you to use it as motivation to address the bigger problem (i.e., the fact that you don't trust your managers). Start by peeling your own onion to get at the root of your manager concern. Do you have too many managers or too many levels? Are they not the right people? Are their goals out of alignment with what's valued by your organization as a whole? I'm not saying that these issues can be fixed quickly or easily; in fact, this may create a completely new agenda item for you. But the fact that you don't trust the capability of your managers has much more far-reaching consequences than its impact on your performance management solution. It's something that you're going to need to address, no matter what. And if you succeed in building that capability in your managers? Then you'll have a powerful team that will take you anywhere you need to go.

Of course, no matter whom you have in place, you'll need to invest in readying your managers for their roles in your new solution. Throughout the story, we've talked about bringing this group along. Like your leaders, they'll need some special attention, especially if the roles they are playing are changing substantially. There are ways in which they may need to let go of some control, like handing the keys to your employees to manage their own careers. Then there are other roles they may need to get comfortable with owning, like determining awards without a numerical indicator. And often they'll need to change their mode of operating from telling to listening and helping. These changes may not be comfortable. No problem—you'll just need to guide them through the change, help them build their capabilities, give them tools to shore them up, and check in from time to time to see how they are doing.

"It's just so weird not to do it."

One of the challenges we face as we try to leave performance reviews and ratings behind is our basic psychology. We are raised in a world in which nearly everything we do is rated or compared with others, from our infancy right through our professional lives. When we're babies, our development is ranked on a percentile basis with other babies. When we start school, our performance is both graded and measured by standardized tests. We're trained from an early age to seek affirmation through those grades, and we learn to accept the notion that our worth can be assigned to us with a number or letter scored against some standard.

It's no surprise that the thought of getting rid of a review system— of kicking that process of standardized evaluation to the curb—is uncomfortable for us. We've lived our whole lives expecting those periodic rankings (and perhaps even relying upon them) to substantiate our own self-worth. That doesn't mean, however, that we actually *need* them or that they are even good for us. But most of us figured out a long time ago that neither our grades in college nor our SAT scores had a damned thing to do with measuring what kind of person we would become or how likely we were to succeed. And, honestly, neither do performance rating systems. Take it to the bank: a good conversation with an employee about how he or she can grow and succeed in your organization is worth a hundred pointless review scores.

"How do we determine rewards without a rating?"

Similarly, I'll bet that many people in your organization will struggle with the *reward equitably* side of your frame. It's the sticky wicket in the triad, especially given our history of pay models and our standard approach to setting compensation. This change will require your compensation team to shift their thinking, which can play out in a lot of different ways. I've witnessed organizations in which the compensation team saw a new performance management solution as an invitation to rethink their overall rewards strategy. But I've also seen compensation teams dig in their heels and bring the whole initiative to a screeching halt. The best way to avoid the latter outcome is to engage the compensation team early in the design process by inviting them to become collaborators in your solution.

You also need to deal with the fact that it's tempting to just put one number in a machine (or spreadsheet) and have another number fall out the other side. This gives us a pass on owning the decision, and it gives us a deceptively black-and-white view in an area that, in reality, can never be anything but gray. It's extremely important that we get people comfortable with the idea that we need to bring ourselves, our human discernment, and our unique points of view into the reward decision process.

What happens if you just don't want to deal with this area, and the comp team, at all? Well, I've seen what can happen when an organization's design solution emphasizes the *desire to drive organizational performance* and *develop people* but leaves *reward equitably* out of the picture entirely. It's sort of like trying to ride a bike without the chain on. You may be able to coast down a hill, but beyond that it just doesn't work. Rewarding equitably is an integral part of a complete solution, and one your people will expect to be included. Don't leave it out of the picture.

"Legal will have a fit!"

We know we need a paper trail to document behavior and performance problems, and we think our annual review cycle does that for us. Too often, though, it doesn't. As I've pointed out, we tend to rate people too leniently, and to downplay or completely gloss over potentially awkward issues. This is one reason why the reviews of underperformers and good performers often read very much the same. The problem is that if a legal issue does arise, or we simply want to take action in response to an employee's behavior or performance, we're caught in a bind between what we really know about that employee's history and a series of reviews that don't appear all *that* bad. This can lead to a messy situation. It's better to avoid this potential pitfall by documenting issues *as they arise.* Then the issues will be fresh and more accurately recorded—giving you a more sound legal footing and a more actionable position overall.

"Why change? Everyone else does it this way!"

While the majority of organizations still use traditional processes, the tide is turning. Today we're seeing respected and forward-thinking organizations trying to *drive organizational performance, develop people,* and *reward equitably* in new ways. In fact, these pioneers have received significant positive exposure for their innovative programs. That attention certainly doesn't hurt their employer brand (a measure of how positively prospective employees view you compared with your competitors). You have a decision to make here: Are you ready to be out front, or would you prefer to wait until your competition has passed you by before you take action? Maybe you have to wait because you feel you have bigger issues to tackle. Or maybe you're simply going to procrastinate until you're finally dragged kicking and screaming into the new world of performance management at some point in the future. But like it or not, the world is changing, and our old accepted practices will eventually crumble under the weight of the research and the evolving expectations of our employees. Lead or follow—the choice is yours.

Build Your Courage

Now that your solution is designed and it's burning a hole in your pocket, take a good hard look in the mirror and strengthen your resolve. Why? Well, as we've just shown, any alteration to traditional performance management is something that many people in your organization, perhaps some of them very high up, might resist like mad. No matter who else you've got on your side, you're still going to have to own this. You'll need to walk confidently into a room and sell this new solution with everything you've got. You'll need to be able to answer objections, guide executives, and face opposition with steely determination and unshakable confidence.

The good news is that you've got an energized team behind you (assuming you've followed my advice from the previous chapters, that is), a team that has helped you assess, design, and plan your solution. Having this core group at your back is a huge asset. But the bad news is that they represent only a small percentage of your organization, so you'll still have your work cut out for you.

Frankly, it's going to take guts to sell this change, and I'm not going to pretend otherwise. Yet I firmly agree with the old adage that most things in life that are worth doing take courage. Even as adults, we're hesitant to risk the figurative bumps and bruises that can result from tackling tough challenges and sudden change. This is where many leaders find themselves foundering. Although they want to navigate a new path, they keep hearing the siren song of the familiar and the safe. Merriam-Webster defines *courage* as "mental or moral strength to venture, persevere, and withstand danger, fear, or difficulty."[9] Change is difficult primarily because it's scary, and it's scary because it stimulates our innate fear of the unknown. The comfort of familiar habits and routines exerts a strong pull on us. No matter how we brace ourselves to change course and sail bravely on toward a new horizon, there still may be a voice in the back of our minds warning, "There be dragons! Turn back before it's too late!"

> *A leader takes people where they want to go. A great leader takes people where they don't necessarily want to go, but ought to be.*
>
> —ROSALYNN CARTER[10]

Ignore that voice. You're at this point in the process because you're convinced beyond a doubt that there's a better way out there. You've done your research, you've got the facts, and you know that your organization desperately needs a new solution. Trust your expertise. Trust your gut. Trust your preparation. Trust your team. Remind yourself of the many valid reasons why you started this journey in the first place. The earth is not flat, there are no dragons, and the course you've set is both right and necessary. Now sail on.

TOOLBOX

Creating Your Custom Design Principles

Purpose
To work together with your design team to create a set of design
principles to serve as the fundamental goals for your new performance
management solution.

Where are we?

Mobilize	*Sketch*	*Configure*	*Build*	*Implement*
Plan, invite participants, and get started	Align on your principles of design	Configure, test, and validate your solution	Build your solution, manage dependencies	Plan the change, implement, and evaluate

- Lead your leaders
- Plan journey
- Invite the right people to the conversation

- Know your starting place
- Understand your destination
- **Align on your design principles**
- Sketch your frame

Crowdsource your design principles

- Configure your solution
  - Brainstorm
  - Select
  - Confirm
  - Configure
- Test your configuration

- Prepare for Build and implementation
  - Capture your solution visually
  - Manage dependencies (internal TM, & external)
  - Define your systems and technology strategy
  - Create your build plan
  - Plan your change
  - Reassess and evolve your timeline
  - Create supporting content
  - Define your sustainability model

Tips and tricks

I'm going to assume that your design team is all together in a room when describing this process. If that's not the case, you can follow the same process, but you'll need to use technology creatively in place of old-fashioned pen and paper.

Process

1. Place flip charts around the room with these headers:
   - Overall
   - Develop People
   - Reward Equitably
   - Drive Organizational Performance

Figure T.1. PM Reboot drivers as flip chart headers.

2. Write each of the questions from the table below on its own large sticky note. Arrange the sticky notes on the appropriate flip chart.

Figure T.2. Design principle questions.

Overall	■ What's the most important outcome? ■ Success means your employees will describe the solution as _____? ■ Success means your managers will describe the solution as _____? ■ The biggest change the team will experience is _____? ■ What will stay the same?
Develop People	■ How will your solution inspire great careers? ■ What words describe the employee experience you will create or reinforce? ■ What three words will describe giving or receiving feedback? ■ What talent challenges or needs do you want your solution to help solve?
Reward Equitably	■ What three words should describe your proposed rewards philosophy? ■ What behaviors do you most want to reward? ■ How will rewards be determined in the future?
Drive Organizational Performance	■ What strategic goals or imperatives will be supported through your solution? ■ What role will the solution play in connecting individuals and teams to the vision, strategy, or operational plans? ■ Name the top three cultural norms you wish to reinforce or introduce. (Is there one or more you're wanting to eliminate?)

Rather than asking everyone to shout out their answers, have the design team members answer the questions on their own, writing each of their answers on a different sticky note. Individuals can provide multiple answers for the same question if they choose, as long as they're on separate sticky notes. Once everyone has answered the questions, ask your team to put their sticky notes under the relevant questions on the relevant flip charts.

Figure T.3. Design principle questions completed.

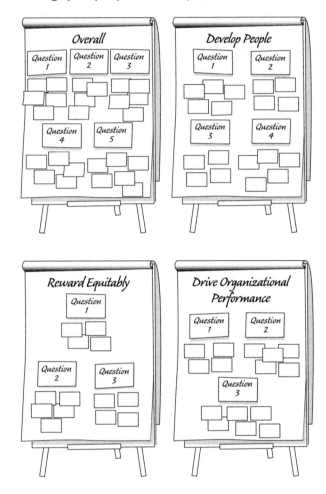

3. When everyone is finished, assign small groups to each of the four flip charts. Have them organize the ideas into clusters of similar answers and then write a statement that describes each of the affinity groups (i.e., clusters) they've created in this way.

Here's an example:

- Let's imagine a team identified these responses as a cluster on the overall flip chart, as shown on the next page.

Figure T.4. Sample responses on sticky notes.

People think the process is easy	People will say it was worth the time spent	Managers say it took less time	Bits of time here and there, not a TON once/yr.
Success = Simple!	Success = stripped down	Success = remove all the "noise"	Stays the same means we honor our lean culture

- Then, for this cluster of responses, the team would write a statement that looked something like this:

Figure T.5. Sample statement on flip chart.

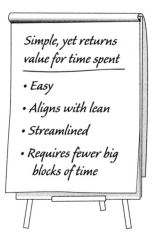

> Simple, yet returns value for time spent
>
> • Easy
> • Aligns with lean
> • Streamlined
> • Requires fewer big blocks of time

4. Once each of the four flip chart teams has clustered and labeled its assigned section, have the teams take turns reporting on their proposed themes. Ask a scribe to capture the drafted statements on a fresh sheet of paper. These are your possible design principles.

5. Now, as a group, step back and look at the list. It's likely that you'll have some overlaps, so take the time to remove redundancies. Work together to consolidate where you can and fine-tune the subheaders to provide more clarity.

6. Once you have a relatively clean list, it's time to set your priorities. Using a multivoting technique, give each design team member six dots and ask them to place their dots on the possible design principles that they feel are most vital to achieving the outcomes you're seeking. If a person wants to place three dots on one design principle, that's OK. It's obviously very important to him or her.

7. Once the votes are in, tally up the totals. Rewrite the top winners in priority order on a clean sheet of paper. If you have more than seven or eight design principles, you'll need to decide as a team where you want to draw the line. Perhaps you can incorporate some of the ideas that got fewer votes into the subheaders of top design principles. Or maybe there are elements that you'll keep in mind but that in the end won't make the top list because other areas are just more important to your organization.

Figure T.6. Sample design principle list.

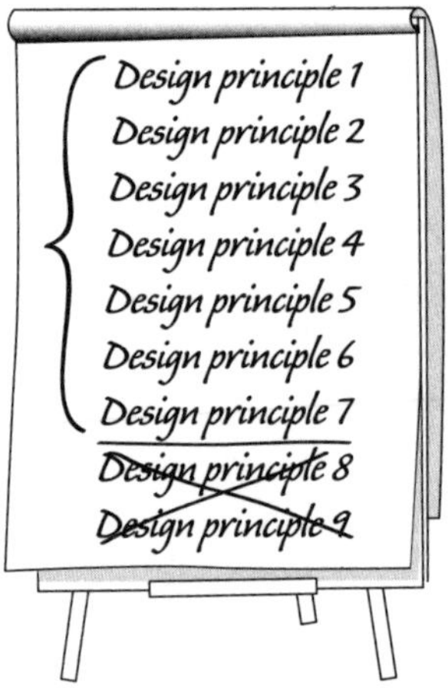

8. How does it look? Check in with the group, and ask yourselves a few questions: Does the group feel that the list of design principles represents the essence of the solution they want to deliver? When a person reads the list, would he or she understand the experience

you're intending to create for your organization? Is anything major missing? Has the team been bold and challenged tradition and old thinking? Are people excited about the list and ready to move to the next step?

9. At this point, I recommend assigning one person the job of typing up the list (in priority order) and distributing it to the group. Take a night or even a day or two and reflect on the principles individually.

10. Now bring the design group back together for a final review and sign-off. And there you have them—your design principles!

Design Principle Worksheet and Sketchpad

Purpose

The following steps will allow you to sketch your performance management frame in order to create a visual representation of how your design principles relate to the Three Common Goals, test which of the Three Common Goals are emphasized most by your design principles, and discuss the interconnectedness among the Three Common Goals.

Where are we?

Mobilize	***Sketch***	*Configure*	*Build*	*Implement*
Plan, invite participants, and get started	Align on your principles of design	Configure, test, and validate your solution	Build your solution, manage dependencies	Plan the change, implement, and evaluate

▪ Lead your leaders
▪ Plan journey
▪ Invite the right people to the conversation
	▪ Know your starting place
	▪ Understand your destination
	▪ Align on your design principles
	▪ **Sketch your frame**
	
	Crowdsource your design principles
		▪ Configure your solution
		  ▫ Brainstorm
		  ▫ Select
		  ▫ Confirm
		  ▫ Configure
		▪ Test your configuration
			▪ Prepare for Build and implementation
			  ▫ Capture your solution visually
			  ▫ Manage dependencies (internal TM, & external)
			  ▫ Define your systems and technology strategy
			  ▫ Create your build plan
			  ▫ Plan your change
			  ▫ Reassess and evolve your timeline
			  ▫ Create supporting content
			  ▫ Define your sustainability model

Tips and tricks

- Be sure your design principles are in prioritized order.

- If one of your design principles is neutral, meaning it doesn't support one Common Goal more than another (I'm thinking something like "Make it simple"), give it a "2" for each goal.

- There is no right or wrong answer when assessing how well your design principles support each goal. The key is to use a consistent method of evaluation.

- For additional worksheets and sketchpads, visit
  www.thePMReboot.com.

Process

Complete the Design Principle Worksheet:

1. Write your design principles in the first column in order of priority
   (see figure T.7).

2. For each row, assess how well your design principle supports the
   common goal. I've added a few notes at the top of each column to
   trigger your thinking. Scoring is simple:

   - High = 3
   - Medium = 2
   - Low = 1
   - Not at all = 0

3. For each cell, multiply the number you've written (your 0–3
   assessment) by the number provided in the cell. Write your answer
   in the shape provided.

4. Once you've completed each cell, add up your three columns.

Now complete the Design Principle Sketchpad:

5. Move on to the Design Principle Sketchpad (see figure T.8) to
   sketch your frame.

6. Write your column totals in the corresponding shape on the
   sketchpad. In other words, note the number total for each of the
   Three Common Goals on the corresponding axis in figure T.8.

7. Graph your three points on the appropriate axis. (For example, if
   your total for the Develop People column was 35, you would put a
   mark on the Develop People axis on the spot that represents 35.)

8. Lightly sketch the connections between the three points to make
   a frame. To decide how thick to make each of the lines, consider
   how related you expect your design to be across the three goals,
   and complete your lines accordingly. As I explained in chapter 6,
   for strong connections, use a thick bold line; for light connections
   use a light (or dotted) line.

Discussion questions

- Does your frame represent what you expected?
- Are the right goals being emphasized?
- If you were to complete this same worksheet with your current process, what would it look like sketched out?

Figure T.7. Design Principle Worksheet.

		○ Drive Organizational Performance	☐ Develop People	◇ Reward Equitably
	Write design principles here, in order of priority	■ Strategy and goal alignment ■ Culture enchancement ■ Strategic communication	■ Career development ■ Retention of top perrformers ■ Leader/manager development	■ Differentiated rewards ■ Promotion and advancements ■ Total rewards and recognition
①		___ X 3 = ○	___ X 3 = ☐	___ X 3 = ◇
②		___ X 3 = ○	___ X 3 = ☐	___ X 3 = ◇
③		___ X 3 = ○	___ X 3 = ☐	___ X 3 = ◇
④		___ X 2 = ○	___ X 2 = ☐	___ X 2 = ◇
⑤		___ X 2 = ○	___ X 2 = ☐	___ X 2 = ◇
⑥		___ X 2 = ○	___ X 2 = ☐	___ X 2 = ◇
⑦		___ X 1 = ○	___ X 1 = ☐	___ X 1 = ◇
⑧		___ X 1 = ○	___ X 1 = ☐	___ X 1 = ◇
	TOTALS	○ ___	☐ ___	◇ ___
High = 3; Medium = 2; Low = 1; None = 0				

Figure T.8. Design Principle Sketchpad.

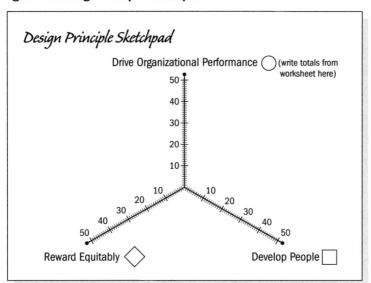

The PM Reboot Sketchbook

Purpose

This section will show you how to use the PM Reboot Sketchbook to do the following:

- Build a visual representation of your own current state and your desired state performance management frames

- Quickly check out what this is all about

- Get a few initial ideas regarding your design principles

We'll also discuss how to use the group version of the PM Reboot Sketchbook to do the following:

- Kick off your design process with the input of each member of your design team

- Invite a broader group of people to the conversation

- Understand which design principles are most valued across a diverse team within your organization

- Test which of the Three Common Goals are most important to each member of your invited group

- Use data and visual insight to support the design conversation with the goal of building an aligned view of your design priorities

Where are we?

Mobilize	*Sketch*	*Configure*	*Build*	*Implement*
Plan, invite participants, and get started	**Align on your principles of design**	Configure, test, and validate your solution	Build your solution, manage dependencies	Plan the change, implement, and evaluate

▪ Lead your leaders ▪ Plan journey ▪ Invite the right people to the conversation	▪ **Know your starting place** ▪ **Understand your destination** ▪ **Align on your design principles** ▪ **Sketch your frame** *Crowdsource your design principles*	▪ Configure your solution ▪ Brainstorm ▪ Select ▪ Confirm ▪ Configure ▪ Test your configuration	▪ Prepare for Build and implementation ▪ Capture your solution visually ▪ Manage dependencies (internal TM, & external) ▪ Define your systems and technology strategy ▪ Create your build plan ▪ Plan your change ▪ Reassess and evolve your timeline ▪ Create supporting content ▪ Define your sustainability model	

Tips and tricks

- HR leaders often use the group sketchbook to kick off the conversation with their executive teams.

- This is a great way to get people thinking and talking.

Process

To make your own sketch:

1. Go to **www.thePMReboot.com** to access the PM Reboot Sketchbook. The tool will prompt you through the following steps.

2. For each question, choose the rating that best describes your current practices. Use this simple scale: 0 = not happening here at all; 1= some people do it / sometimes; 2 = rock solid— it's how we operate. We've selected these twelve questions from our larger set of current state assessment questions to give you a quick idea of your starting place.

The Sketchbook will ask you to pick from a list of "prepackaged" design principles. Your job is to simply choose your top six. (For this purpose, we created nineteen design principles that are commonly used by organizations rebooting their performance management solution. While they will definitely help you test alignment, they are not the design principles you created and therefore aren't customized to your organization. Using your own design principles is always best!)

3. Select "generate." It generates your current and desired state performance management frames, based on your selections.

To sketch with a group, you can use our fee-based online tool:

1. If you're interested in inviting more people to the conversation, upgrade to the multiuser version of the PM Reboot Sketchbook. Invite the people you'd like to participate—and you'll be off and running.

2. The Sketchbook will automatically send an email invitation to the group you've identified. Once they've completed their sketches, you'll be able to view the results and generate summary reports.

3. The architecture of their individual performance frames will give you insights into how well your group is aligned on the design principles and common goals that they think are most important.

Discussion questions

- How aligned is the group? Does that alignment give you a solid foundation on which to begin your design conversation?

- Does your group agree on which of the Three Common Goals is most important? If not, how diverse are their opinions?

- Do you agree on your starting place? If not, why not?

- How would you write your own design principles to bring the group together?

Crowdsourcing Your Design Principles

Purpose

To show the value of crowdsourcing your design principles through an example.

Where are we?

Mobilize	*Sketch*	*Configure*	*Build*	*Implement*
Plan, invite participants, and get started	**Align on your principles of design**	Configure, test, and validate your solution	Build your solution, manage dependencies	Plan the change, implement, and evaluate

▪ Lead your leaders	▪ **Know your starting place**	▪ Configure your solution	▪ Prepare for Build and implementation	
▪ Plan journey	▪ **Understand your destination**	▫ Brainstorm	▫ Capture your solution visually	
▪ Invite the right people to the conversation	▪ **Align on your design principles**	▫ Select	▫ Manage dependencies (internal TM, & external)	
	▪ **Sketch your frame**	▫ Confirm	▫ Define your systems and technology strategy	
		▫ Configure	▫ Create your build plan	
	Crowdsource your design principles	▪ Test your configuration	▫ Plan your change	
			▫ Reassess and evolve your timeline	
			▫ Create supporting content	
			▫ Define your sustainability model	

The story

At PeopleFirm, we took a team of seven through our crowdsourcing version of the PM Reboot Sketchbook, at **www.thePMReboot.com**. The results of their selections are shown in figure T.9, and each column represents a participant in the conversation. This illustrates where the group is aligned and where they are not. Interestingly, only one design principle in our example here was selected by almost everyone, meaning that only one design principle had strong alignment across the group. Just one! Three design principles were not selected by anyone, and five had only one vote, which shows us that the group has a level of alignment on what's *not* important to them. But that leaves ten design principles that received only two to four votes out of the seven. That's not what I'd call alignment. Looks like there's still some work to do!

Figure T.9. Team aggregate example.

FUTURE STATE PRINCIPLE	TOTAL	Doc	Grumpy	Happy	Sleepy	Bashful	Sneezy	Dopey	ALIGNMENT
Principle M	6								
Principle J	4								
Principle G	4								
Principle D	4								
Principle I	3								
Principle F	3								
Principle C	3								
Principle E	3								
Principle B	3								
Principle A	2								
Principle R	2								
Principle O	1								
Principle L	1								
Principle Q	1								
Principle N	1								
Principle K	1								
Principle H	0								
Principle S	0								
Principle P	0								

Now that the team knew each person's design preferences, they took the alignment assessment one step further by sketching their individual performance management frames. Just as any picture paints a thousand words, these sketches give us a visual read on how each member of our group of seven was leaning regarding the Three Common Goals: *drive organizational performance, develop people,* and *reward equitably.* These sketched representations of their design priorities allow us to compare the person-to-person similarities and differences of their PM frames.

This provides greater understanding of the participants' selections. It is possible that several people might select different design principles and therefore not appear aligned at first glance, but when you sketch out their frames, you could find that they all support a similar agenda (such as placing more emphasis on rewarding equitably). You've now learned that the group is more aligned than you initially thought. In short, taking this extra step gives you greater insights into the perspectives of others, while providing a visual platform to support group discussion and alignment.

When we aggregate the responses of the seven members of this group, the collective frame looks like the sketch in figure T.10. Note that it appears to be leaning more toward drive organizational performance and develop people (you can tell because those goals are farther out along their axes).

Figure T.10. Design Principle Sketchpad.

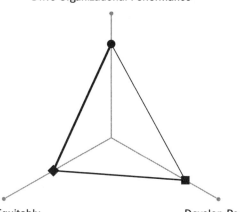

Drive Organizational Performance

Reward Equitably   Develop People

Now let's look at a couple of individuals' unique responses (see figure T.11). Check out the difference! Doc leans strongly toward reward equitably, while Happy does the same toward develop people. Examining individual frames gives us more insight into each participant's view of the direction in which he or she would like to see your future solution go. In this case, we can conclude that Doc and Happy have some things to talk about before they get into the nitty-gritty design details of their PM solution.

Figure T.11. Sample team member frames.

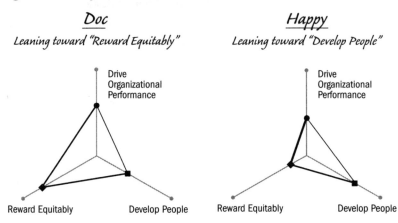

I hope our simple online sketchbook spotlights where tradeoffs or compromises might be required across any size team. It can give you a lens into people's thoughts and preferences in a matter of a few minutes. If nothing else, it's sure to get people thinking and talking.

Configuration Checklist

Purpose

The Configuration Checklist is used to help you think through your options when you're in the Configure stage. Use it to:

- Confirm the PM Practices you've selected
- Explore other ideas you may not have considered

Where are we?

Mobilize	*Sketch*	**Configure**	*Build*	*Implement*
Plan, invite participants, and get started	Align on your principles of design	Configure, test, and validate your solution	Build your solution, manage dependencies	Plan the change, implement, and evaluate

- Lead your leaders
- Plan journey
- Invite the right people to the conversation

- Know your starting place
- Understand your destination
- Align on your design principles
- Sketch your frame

Crowdsource your design principles

- **Configure your solution**
  - Brainstorm
  - Select
  - **Confirm**
  - Configure
- **Test your configuration**

- Prepare for Build and implementation
  - Capture your solution visually
  - Manage dependencies (internal TM, & external)
  - Define your systems and technology strategy
  - Create your build plan
  - Plan your change
  - Reassess and evolve your timeline
  - Create supporting content
  - Define your sustainability model

Tips and tricks

- Feel free to pick more than one of the PM Practices for any of the configuration categories.
- Consider addressing different specific employee segments with variations in your approach.

- Check in on those practices that make up your current performance program. Get clear on if they will remain, be modified, or eliminated.

- Use this time to consider whether you've been bold enough with your choices.

Process

As a team, walk through each of the configuration categories. Discuss the options you've already chosen. Consider if you've missed something or would like to use a different PM Practice than the one you initially selected. These are suggestions only; use this tool to drive discussions among your team about the PM Practices that will make up your final solution (see figure T.12).

Figure T.12. Configuration Checklist.

CONFIGURATION CATEGORY	PM PRACTICES OPTIONS
Goals and Alignment	■ Cascaded goals (inherited or optional) ■ Shared goals (manager/team) ■ Individual targets ■ Project or event goals ■ Commitments ■ Development goals
Feedback and Performance Insights	■ Self-assessment ■ Manager or supervisor assessment ■ Peer or team feedback ■ Informal, in the moment
Coaching and Mentoring	■ Manager/supervisor as coach ■ Formal mentoring ■ External coaches ■ Peer or team feedback ■ Informal, in the moment
Career and Development Planning	■ Integrated career planning with feedback process ■ Standalone development plans and programs ■ Aligned to company goals ■ Aligned to career aspirations—future roles ■ Aligned with competency models/behaviors

CONFIGURATION CATEGORY	PM PRACTICES OPTIONS
Talent Reviews and Insights	▪ None
	▪ HR audit of assessment to test biases
	▪ TR to assess relative performance
	▪ TR to identify differentiated performance
	▪ TR to support succession and workforce planning
	▪ TR to assess retention and performance risks
	▪ TR to inform compensation decisions and reward strategies
Total Rewards	▪ Base pay—capabilities aligned
	▪ Base pay—role aligned
	▪ Wide salary bands
	▪ Narrow bands or targed by role
	▪ Merit increases
	▪ Bonus program
	▪ Recognition program

Configuration Worksheet and Sketchpad

Purpose

Re-sketch your performance management frame to test your configuration by doing the following:

- Create a visual representation of how your configured solution relates to the Three Common Goals.

- Test if you've stayed true to your desired architecture and areas of emphasis.

- Explore the interconnections among the Three Common Goals.

- Encourage your design team to validate their configured solution before moving forward.

Where are we?

Mobilize	*Sketch*	*Configure*	*Build*	*Implement*
Plan, invite participants, and get started	Align on your principles of design	Configure, test, and validate your solution	Build your solution, manage dependencies	Plan the change, implement, and evaluate
▪ Lead your leaders	▪ Know your starting place	▪ Configure your solution	▪ Prepare for Build and implementation	
▪ Plan journey	▪ Understand your destination	▪ Brainstorm	▫ Capture your solution visually	
▪ Invite the right people to the conversation	▪ Align on your design principles	▪ Select	▫ Manage dependencies (internal TM, & external)	
		▪ Confirm	▫ Define your systems and technology strategy	
	▪ Sketch your frame	▪ Configure	▫ Create your build plan	
		▪ **Test your configuration**	▫ Plan your change	
	Crowdsource your design principles		▫ Reassess and evolve your timeline	
			▫ Create supporting content	
			▫ Define your sustainability model	

Tips and tricks

- There is no right or wrong answer when assessing how well your design principles support each goal. The key is to use a consistent method of evaluation.

Configuration Worksheet steps:

1. Summarize your solution against the six configuration categories by writing your chosen PM Practices under the appropriate category (see figure T.13).

2. For each configuration category (row), assess how well your design is supporting the common goals. Score as you did before:

   a. High = 3

   b. Medium = 2

   c. Low = 1

   d. Not at all = 0

3. Once you've completed the table, add up your three columns.

Configuration Sketchpad steps:

4. Move to the Configuration Sketchpad (see figure T.14) to sketch your frame.

5. As you did when sketching your design principles, write your column totals in the corresponding shape on the sketchpad. In other words, note the number total for each of the three goals on its corresponding axis.

6. Graph your three points on the appropriate axis.

7. Sketch in your lines based on how interconnected your solution is across the three goals. Again, for strong connections, use a thick bold line; for light connections, use a light (or dotted) line.

Discussion questions

- How do your frames compare?

- Have you stayed true to your intent?

- Have you reached far enough? Have you made bold choices that will create your desired experience for employees and managers?

- Are you happy with your solution design?

Figure T.13. Configuration Worksheet.

		○ *Drive Organizational Performance*	☐ *Develop People*	◇ *Reward Equitably*
	Summarize your PM Practices for each configuration category	■ Strategy and goal alignment ■ Culture enhancement ■ Strategic communication	■ Career development ■ Retention of top perrformers ■ Leader/manager development	■ Differentiated rewards ■ Promotion and advancements ■ Total rewards and recognition
①	*Goals and alignments*			
②	*Feedback and performance insights*			
③	*Coaching and mentoring*			
④	*Career and development planning*			
⑤	*Talent Reviews (TR) and insights*			
⑥	*Total rewards*			
	TOTALS	○ ___	☐ ___	◇ ___

High = 3; Medium = 2; Low = 1; None = 0

Figure T.14. Configuration Sketchpad.

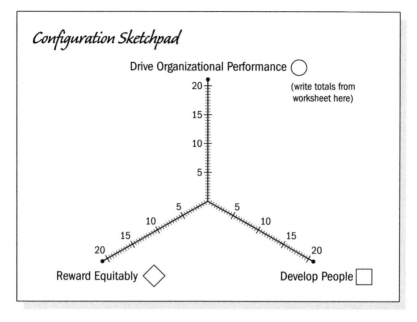

Guide to Creating Your Change Plan

Purpose

Create a comprehensive change plan to guide your change management efforts. Plan how you will build awareness, understanding, and buy-in for your new PM solution across all impacted people. A great change plan considers the following questions:

- Who will be impacted by this change—your stakeholder groups?

- What is the nature of the changes that each of your stakeholder groups will experience?

- When should you engage each stakeholder group, and where do you want them along the change curve over time?

- How much support and information is needed for each stakeholder group?

Where are we?

Mobilize	*Sketch*	*Configure*	**Build**	*Implement*
Plan, invite participants, and get started	Align on your principles of design	Configure, test, and validate your solution	Build your solution, manage dependencies	Plan the change, implement, and evaluate

• Lead your leaders	▪ Know your starting place	• Configure your solution	▪ Prepare for Build and implementation
▪ Plan journey	▪ Understand your destination	• Brainstorm	• Capture your solution visually
▪ Invite the right people to the conversation	▪ Align on your design principles	• Select	• Manage dependencies (internal TM, & external)
	▪ Sketch your frame	• Confirm	• Define your systems and technology strategy
		• Configure	• Create your build plan
	Crowdsource your design principles	▪ Test your configuration	**• Plan your change**
			• Reassess and evolve your timeline
			• Create supporting content
			• Define your sustainability model

Tips and tricks

1. When you're creating your change plan, don't forget that you need to share it! Typically, change plans can get pretty complex, but the last thing people will want to look at is a huge Excel spreadsheet. Rather, use visuals to show how you will move key stakeholders through the change curve. Consider creating a shareable version that fits on one sheet of paper, even if it's a large sheet. Your object is to make the plan quick and easy to understand.

2. Stuff happens and things change, so keep it current and adapt it as needed.

Steps to create your change plan

1. Grab yourself a big piece of paper, perhaps a flip chart or a roll of butcher paper.

2. Down the left side of your paper, add the key stakeholder groups you have identified, using sticky notes. (I like to jot down the degree of impact we assessed for each group on that sticky note as well. In fact, you might want to list them by impact.)

3. Along the top of your paper, put your timeline, showing the months and weeks until you go live with your new solution. Add any notable milestones on your timeline, things like the CEO State of the Union address, completion of strategic planning for the coming year, or an upcoming busy season you want to highlight.

4. Now you need to ponder the change curve* in relationship to each of your stakeholder groups. In other words, consider where you need them to be in their change process at each point in your timeline. Recognize that everyone doesn't need to be in the same place at the same time. Perhaps you wish to bring two groups through the curve ahead of others, such as your leaders and your HR business partners (since you need these groups with you before you go too far with the rest of the organization). Work with your design team to discuss how you might stage your approach and what areas need your greatest focus.

* Need more information about the change curve? See "Understanding the Change Curve" at **thePMReboot.com/toolkit.**

5. Now start adding your ideas for how you're going to get them there. Perhaps you kick off by bringing in an external speaker to talk with your critical stakeholders. Or maybe you plan to design a campaign strategy that will build excitement and momentum over time. Midway through your plan, consider an open house to let people walk through the process and tools, ask questions, and engage in a fun and positive environment. Give lots of thought to readiness, which may be manager training, or testing elements of your design to engage and prepare people (this also gives you insights into how to make it better or easier). There are hundreds of ideas. The key is understanding whom you need to reach with what information, and what level of preparedness fits best within the constraints of time and money. When you've finished this exercise, you should have a good version 1 of your change plan.

6. Once you've got this high-level plan, then you can begin to build it out. I like to build a fairly detailed project outline that shows each activity in the change plan and notes scope, timing, audience, deliverables, success criteria, and, where possible, measurement.

Final Thoughts

AS DAVE ULRICH POINTS OUT IN the foreword, this book is not a magic pill guaranteed to instantly cure your performance management headache; I've given you something much richer instead. You see, there's an invaluable side benefit to this whole process. Once you've gone through it with your design team and your organization, you'll be stronger and more capable than you ever could have imagined. You'll have developed a knowledge of yourself, of your organization, of your corporate strategy, and of how that strategy can and should be expressed through performance management (or something you'll probably no longer call performance management!). Yes, you'll have a solution in place that is literally custom-made for your organization and thoughtfully designed and implemented. But that's not all. Since you built it, you'll also have the skill set to improve on the original, to adapt, to edit, and to keep your performance management relevant no matter where your organization might go or what might change in the world.

One recurring theme you may have noticed as you read this book is that this process isn't about *things*. It's not about computer software, surveys, review forms, or process plans. No, the real key to this whole thing is *people*. It's about talking to them, listening to them, engaging them, trusting them, and, above all, never losing sight of the fact that the process must serve them and not the other way around. (Have you figured out yet why we named our company PeopleFirm?) We need to bring more humanity into the workplace, and rethinking performance management is the perfect vehicle to do just that.

The Last Competitive Frontier

Speaking of people and culture, I simply cannot write a book on performance management without leaving you with these two final thoughts. The first is this: *the last competitive business frontier is our people.* Working as a management consultant for the last quarter of a century, moving in and out of so many organizations and observing a wide array of cultures and management styles, has afforded me an interesting perspective. And from that unique fly-on-the-wall position, certain things have become very clear.

I've staked my own career and my company's reputation on one critical idea: that people (not technology, not some newfangled management system, not your product or service, but people) are the one thing that can make your company stand out in a crowd. Advances in Web- and cloud-based applications have created a far more equal footing for organizations of all shapes and sizes. This means that technology is not the key differentiator it once was. Even things like strategy, product, marketing, and service all come down to people. The winning organizations are and will continue to be those that have the best people working as a team and aligned to a clear direction. Making that happen must be your top priority. If you've hired good ones and give them the tools they need, your people will be ready and willing to step up, as long as you're willing to get out of their way.

You've surely noted that a foundational theme in my approach is trust, so you should not be surprised to learn that I'm asking you to do something that is contrary to how many of us have been taught to manage, which is simply learning to let go and trust your people.

As scary as it is to relinquish control a bit, it's what we have to do in order to successfully drive performance and attract and keep the best people. It's time to embrace a new world of trust, shared goals, diverse voices, and transparency. Only then will we gain full value from that last competitive resource.

Performance Management as a Driver of Culture Change

Nowadays I'm asked to address culture change more than ever before. Many organizations want to keep some elements of their culture while shedding bad habits or limiting behaviors, or maybe add a few new norms to optimize how they operate as a team and change the experience of working day to day. Well, here's another great thing about this process I've taken you through: the performance management solution you design can send a very strong signal to your team about the kind of culture you are seeking to drive. The very flexibility of building a custom solution for your organization—and *only* your organization— means that you can be extraordinarily tactical about driving the culture you want.

Of course, this knife cuts both ways. Too often, leaders fail to consider the cultural signals they are sending with their current performance management tactics. If you stake a claim on a certain type of culture (say, one flush with trust and transparency), and your performance management approach sends the opposite message by, for instance, keeping some parts of the system hidden from the participants, you'll struggle to make real progress toward achieving that new ideal. Performance management plays a critical role in signaling what is expected, important, and valued in an organization. Don't believe me? Just sit down at a table full of employees at lunch and ask for their performance management stories. For almost all employees, new and old, in whatever role, the performance management process is a rich topic of conversation, often for all the wrong reasons.

Culture is tricky and powerful stuff. At PeopleFirm, we define it simply as "the way we do things around here." I frequently quote Shawn Parr's assertion from a *Fast Company* article that "[c]ulture is the environment in which your strategy and your brand thrives or *dies a slow death*" (italics mine).[1] That may sound like an overstatement, but I've seen for myself how culture can literally make the difference between a healthy and robust organization and one that's on life support.

If culture change is one of your goals, be sure to keep that goal in mind from the very beginning of the design process. Know what cultural signals you *don't* want to send, and capture the signals you *do* want to send in your design principles. It's important enough that you need to make sure that it influences your thinking from day one.

Let's Stay in Touch

I've done my best to give you the reasons for change and the tools to make it happen, and now the rest is up to you. Honestly, it feels a bit like I'm pushing you out of the nest, and even though I'm confident that you've got everything you need to take flight on your own, I also know that you don't need to fly solo. Many others are ready to make the same leap you're contemplating. They want to ditch their old performance management ways and blaze the trail to a brave new world—but so many think they have to go it alone. It's especially bad if you're the lone prophet in a more, shall we say, old-fashioned organization. This can be a daunting prospect at best, and at worst, a terrifying one. So, in keeping with the premise that when the going gets tough, the tough find a community, I'd like to propose that those of us who are passionate about rebooting performance management gather a group of like-minded folks. I'm envisioning a place of discussion where people can hear what others are doing, offer support, ask questions, and learn from (and be inspired by) one another's successes.

With that in mind, I've created a *PM Reboot* group on LinkedIn. Please consider joining it to post your questions, suggestions, failures, lessons learned, and critiques. The only ground rule is no sales—the last thing we want to do is waste anyone's time. Everything else is fair game. Remember that I don't have all the answers, and to tell you the truth, that's one of the reasons why I want to hear your thoughts and ideas. In the end, I hope to learn as much from the conversation as you do. Together we can share our experiences to create a community of support and a forum for exciting, groundbreaking ideas.

My last bit of advice? Remember that Rome was not built in a day. It's a dusty phrase, of course, but one that I've always liked. Don't get me wrong—I'm as impatient as anyone. I love the exhilaration of scribbling madly on whiteboards with a bunch of my colleagues in a conference room, brainstorming, debating, sharing knowledge and ideas and more than a few laughs as we create something amazing together—something that turns out to be smart, effective, and elegant, and immeasurably better than anything any of us could have come up with on our own. That's my idea of fun, and it's what I live for in my professional life. But eager as I am to see how the fruits of our labor play out, I've come to realize that the full value of what we've created doesn't show itself in the first few days or weeks that follow. The *real* success happens when that work evolves into something tangible that takes root permanently in an organization. Therein lies the payoff, and it doesn't happen overnight or without a healthy share of headaches and heartaches. I remind myself often that change is a process, not an event. Patience and perseverance are required, sometimes in great abundance.

> *The cost of being wrong is less than the cost of doing nothing.*
> —SETH GODIN, *POKE THE BOX*[2]

So I can't promise that all will go smoothly as you reboot your performance management solution; in fact, I can promise that it won't. All you can do is commit to choosing the right solution for your organization and do your damnedest to make sure that everyone's on board; then take a deep breath and start living the change. If things are a little wobbly at first, don't panic: the same tools you used to build your little beauty can also be used to tweak things as you go. Whatever you do, no matter how many bumps you hit along the way, trust yourself, trust your people, and trust the process. Above all, keep moving forward, and never, ever look back.

Happy rebooting.

Notes

Chapter 1: Welcome to the PM Reboot

1. "On Performance," Integrating Performance, accessed February 8, 2015, http://www.integratingperformance.com.

2. Peter Cappelli, "Should Performance Reviews Be Fired?" Wharton Center for Human Resources, April 27, 2011, accessed February 8, 2015, http://knowledge. wharton.upenn.edu/article/should-performance-reviews-be-fired/.

3. Society for Human Resource Management, accessed February 8, 2015, https://www.insala.com/Articles/performance-management-software/ performance-management-current-trends.asp.

4. Sylvia Vorhauser-Smith, "Three Reasons Performance Management Will Change in 2013," *Forbes,* December 16, 2012, http://www.forbes.com/sites/ sylviavorhausersmith/2012/12/16/the-new-face-of-performance-management- trading-annual-reviews-for-agile-management/.

5. Eric Mosley, "Performance Management Meets the Wisdom of Crowds," Globoforce, 2012, accessed February 8, 2015, http://www.engagementstrategiesonline.com/ Performance-Management-Meets-the-Wisdom-of-Crowds/.

6. Mark Murphy, "The 3 Reasons Employees Hate Performance Reviews," Leadership IQ, May 1, 2012, http://www.hr.com/en/app/blog/2012/05/ leadership-iq-article--the-3-reasons-employees-hat_h1p3ce7e.html.

7. Cliff Stevenson, "Performance Management: Sticking with What Doesn't Work," i4CP TrendWatchers, October 31, 2013, Issue 583, http://www.i4cp.com/ trendwatchers/2013/10/31/performance-management-sticking-with-what- doesn-t-work.

8. David Rock, Josh Davis, and Beth Jones, "Kill Your Performance Ratings: Neuroscience Shows Why Numbers-Based HR Management Is Obsolete," *Strategy+Business,* issue 76 (Autumn 2014), http://www.strategy-business.com/ media/file/00275_Kill_Your_Perfomance_Ratings.pdf.

9. Ray Williams, "Why CEOs need to scrap employee reviews," *Psychology Today,* May 17, 2011, accessed February 8, 2015, https://www.psychologytoday.com/ blog/wired-success/201105/why-ceos-need-scrap-employee-performance- reviews.

Chapter 2: The Eight Fatal Flaws

1. Daniel Pink, "The Puzzle of Motivation," TED Talk, July 2009, accessed February 8, 2015, http://www.ted.com/talks/dan_pink_on_motivation.html.

2. Daniel H. Pink, *Drive: The Surprising Truth About What Motivates Us* (New York: Riverhead Books, 2011).

3. David Rock et al., "Kill Your Performance Ratings."

4. Dick Richards, *Artful Work: Awakening Joy, Meaning, and Commitment in the Workplace* (San Francisco: Berrett-Koehler Publishers, 1995), 65.

5. David Rock et al., "Lead change with the brain in mind," *NeuroLeadership Journal,* issue 4, http://www.davidrock.net/files/07_Lead_change_with_the_brain_in_mind_US.pdf; David Rock, Your Brain at Work (New York: HarperCollins, 2009), http://www.your-brain-at-work.com/.

6. Josh Bersin, "The Myth of the Bell Curve: Look for the Hyper-Performers," *Forbes,* February 19, 2014, accessed February 8, 2015, http://http://www.forbes.com/sites/joshbersin/2014/02/19/the-myth-of-the-bell-curve-look-for-the-hyper-performers/.

7. Rick Maurer, *Tools for Giving Feedback* (Portland OR: Productivity Press, 1994), 51.

8. Samuel Culbert and Lawrence Rout, *Get Rid of the Performance Review!: How Companies Can Stop Intimidating, Start Managing—and Focus on What Really Matters* (New York: Business Plus, 2010).

9. Cappelli, "Should Performance Reviews Be Fired?"

10. Marcus Buckingham, "Putting the Strengths-Based Perspective to Work," the Marcus Buckingham Company (TMBC), 2010, p. 2, accessed February 8, 2015, http://jimseybert.com/wp-content/uploads/2010/09/TMBC-Strengths-White-Paper_JS.pdf.

11. Vauhini Vara, "The Push Against Performance Reviews," *New Yorker,* July 24, 2015, http://www.newyorker.com/business/currency/the-push-against-performance-reviews.

12. Tony Schwartz, "The Only Thing That Really Matters," *Harvard Business Review,* June 1, 2011, https://hbr.org/2011/06/the-only-thing-that-really-mat.html.

13. Tom Coens and Mary Jenkins, *Abolishing Performance Appraisals: Why They Backfire and What to Do Instead* (San Francisco: Berrett-Koehler Publishers, 2002), 93.

14. Mark de Rond, "Always Rely on a Team, Not Individuals," *Forbes,* August 5, 2010, accessed February 8, 2015, http://www.forbes.com/2010/08/05/teams-teamwork-individuals-leadership-managing-collaboration.html.

15. Culbert and Rout, *Get Rid of the Performance Review!,* 63.

16. Marcus Buckingham, "Most HR Data Is Bad Data," *Harvard Business Review,* February 9, 2015, https://hbr.org/2015/02/most-hr-data-is-bad-data.

17. John Smith, "The Traditional Rating Scale: Needs Improvement," *Employee Performance & Talent Management,* February 22, 2011, http://www.employee-performance.com/blog/the-traditional-rating-scale-needs-improvement/.

18. CRG emPerform, "Does Your Performance Rating Scale Need Improvement?" *Employee Performance & Talent Management,* May 6, 2014, accessed February 8, 2015, http://www.employee-performance.com/blog/does-your-performance-rating-scale-need-improvement/.

19. Peter Block, in foreword to Tom Coens and Mary Jenkins, *Abolishing Performance Appraisals: Why They Backfire and What to Do Instead* (San Francisco: Berrett-Koehler Publishers, 2000), xiii.

20. Alfie Kohn, *Punished by Rewards: The Trouble with Gold Stars, Incentive Plans, A's, Praise, and Other Bribes* (New York: Mariner Books, 1999), 56.

21. Pink, *Drive.*

22. Alfie Kohn and Jennifer Powell, "How incentives undermine performance," *Journal for Quality and Participation* 21, no. 2 (March–April 1998): 8.

23. Nina Gupta and Atul Mitra, "The Value of Financial Incentives: Myths and Empirical Realities," *ACA Journal* 7, no. 3 (Autumn 1998): 62, http://www.researchgate.net/publication/274719227_The_value_of_ financial_incentives_Myths_and_empirical_realities.

24. Martin Dewhurst, Matthew Guthridge, and Elizabeth Mohr, "Motivating people: Getting beyond money," *McKinsey Quarterly,* November 2009, accessed February 8, 2015, http://www.mckinsey.com/insights/organization/motivating_people_ getting_beyond_money.

25. Murphy, "The 3 Reasons Employees Hate Performance Reviews."

26. W. Edwards Deming, *Out of the Crisis,* "Deadly Disease #3—Evaluation of Performance, Merit Rating, or Annual Review" (Cambridge, MA: MIT Press, 2000), 102.

Chapter 3: The Eight Fundamental Shifts

1. John Maynard Keynes, *The General Theory of Employment, Interest, and Money* (CreateSpace Independent Publishing Platform, November 15, 2011).

2. Jessica DuBois-Maahs, "Should Salaries Be Transparent?" Talent Management, December 12, 2013, accessed February 8, 2015, http://www.talentmgt.com/ articles/should-salaries-be-transparent.

3. Attributed to US Supreme Court Justice Louis Brandeis, accessed February 8, 2015, http://www.brandeis.edu/legacyfund/bio.html.

4. Susan Scott, *Fierce Leadership: A Bold Alternative to the Worst "Best" Practices of Business Today* (New York: Crown Business, 2011).

5. Pink, *Drive.*

6. What's Working study, Mercer, 2011, http://www.slideshare.net/PingElizabeth/ mercer-whats-working-research.

7. Pink, *Drive.*

8. "Six Hidden Enemies That Threaten to Undermine Post-Recession Corporate Performance," Executive Conference Board, 2010, http://www.prweb.com/ releases/CEB/ExecutiveGuidance2010/prweb2974314.htm.

9. Samuel A. Culbert, "Get Rid of the Performance Review!" *Wall Street Journal,* October 20, 2008, http://www.wsj.com/articles/SB122426318874844933.

10. Beverly Kay and Sharon Jordan-Evans, *Love 'Em Or Lose 'Em* (Oakland, California: Berrett-Koehler Publishers, 2014).

11. "2013 SHRM/Globoforce Employee Recognition Survey," Globoforce, May 29, 2013, accessed September 11, 2015, http://www.globoforce.com/news/press-releases/shrmgloboforce-survey-reveals-new-insights/.

12. Scott, *Fierce Leadership.*

13. John R. Childress and Larry E. Senn, *The Secret of a Winning Culture* (Provo, Utah: Executive Excellence Publishing, 2002).

14. Pink, *Drive.*

15. As quoted in Kohn, *Punished by Rewards,* 122.

16. Fred C. Lunenburg, "Goal-Setting Theory of Motivation," *International Journal of Management, Business, and Administration* 15, no. 1 (2011), accessed February 8, 2015, http://www.nationalforum.com/Electronic%20Journal%20Volumes/Lunenburg,%20Fred%20C.%20Goal-Setting%20Theoryof%20Motivation%20IJMBA%20V15%20N1%202011.pdf.

17. Simon Sinek, "Why good leaders make you feel safe," TED Talk, March 2014. http://www.ted.com/talks/simon_sinek_why_good_leaders_make_you_feel_safe?language=en.

18. Tomas Chamorro-Premuzic, "Does Money Really Affect Motivation? A Review of the Research," *Harvard Business Review,* April 2013, accessed February 8, 2015, https://hbr.org/2013/04/does-money-really-affect-motiv.

Chapter 4: The Three Common Goals

1. WorldatWork and Sibson Consulting, 2010 Study on the State of Performance Management, October 2010, accessed February 8, 2015, http://www.worldatwork.org/waw/adimLink?id=44473.

2. Bersin, "The Myth of the Bell Curve."

3. Scott Bohannon, "Six Enemies of Post-Recession Performance," Executive Conference Board Presentation, October 14, 2010, p. 21, http://www.cebglobal.com/exbd/executive-guidance/archive/index.page.

4. Susan Sorenson, "How Employee Engagement Drives Growth," *Gallup Business Journal,* June 20, 2013, accessed February 8, 2015, http://www.gallup.com/businessjournal/163130/employee-engagement-drives-growth.aspx.

5. Towers Watson, 2012 Global Workforce Study: Engagement at Risk—Driving Strong Performance in a Volatile Global Environment, accessed February 8, 2015, http://www.towerswatson.com/assets/pdf/2012-Towers-Watson-Global-Workforce-Study.pdf.

6. Kevin Kruse, "Employee Engagement: The Wonder Drug for Customer Satisfaction," *Forbes,* January 7, 2014, accessed February 8, 2015, http://www.forbes.com/sites/kevinkruse/2014/01/07/employee-engagement-the-wonder-drug-for-customer-satisfaction/.

7. WorldatWork and Sibson Consulting, 2010 Study on the State of Performance Management.

8. CEB, Executive Guidance for 2013: Breakthrough Performance in the New Work Environment, accessed February 8, 2015, http://www.executiveboard.com/exbd-resources/pdf/executive-guidance/eg2013-annual-final.pdf.

9. Carol Morrison, "How to Align Your Employees to Strategic and Business Goals," I4CP Productivity Blog, October 31, 2014, accessed February 8, 2015, http://www.i4cp.com/productivity-blog/2014/10/31/how-to-align-your-employees-to-strategic-and-business-goals.

10. Louis Efron, "Six Reasons Your Best Employees Quit You," Forbes, June 24, 2013, accessed February 8, 2015, http://www.forbes.com/sites/louisefron/2013/06/24/six-reasons-your-best-employees-quit-you/.

Chapter 5: Mobilize

1. Prosci, Inc. Best Practices in Change Management—2014 Edition, p. 4, accessed February 28, 2015, http://offers.prosci.com/research/Prosci-2014-Best-Practices-Executive-Overview.pdf.

2. Stephen R. Covey, author of *The 7 Habits of Highly Effective People* (New York: Simon & Schuster, 2013): "Habit 2: Begin with the End in Mind," https://www.stephencovey.com/7habits/7habits-habit2.php.

3. Frank Kalman, "Adobe Checks In with Performance Conversations," Talent Management, August 22, 2014, accessed February 8, 2015, http://www.talentmgt.com/articles/6719-adobe-check-ins.

Chapter 8: Making It Real

1. Shannon Taylor, "Confronting Challenges Related to Performance in Nonprofit Organizations," University of Georgia, accessed February 24, 2015, http://www.uga.edu/nonprofit/Academics/StudentDocs/Challenge.doc.

2. Marc Lindenberg, "Are We at the Cutting Edge or the Blunt Edge? Improving NGO Organizational Performance with Private and Public Sector Management Frameworks," *Nonprofit Management and Leadership* 11, issue 3 (2001): 255.

3. John C. Sawhill and David Williamson, "Mission Impossible? Measuring Success in Nonprofit Organizations," *Nonprofit Management and Leadership* 11, issue 3 (Spring 2001): 371–86.

4. Peter Drucker, *The Essential Drucker: The Best of Sixty Years of Peter Drucker's Essential Writings on Management* (New York: HarperBusiness, 2003).

5. Geert Hofstede, *Culture's Consequences: Comparing Values, Behaviors, Institutions, and Organizations Across Nations* (London, UK: Sage Publications, 2003).

Chapter 10: Making It Stick

1. Prosci, "Importance of Change Management," accessed February 8, 2015, http://www.prosci.com/change-management/why-change-management/.

2. Prosci, "Change Management Tutorial," accessed February 8, 2015, http://www.change-management.com/tutorial-case-mod3.htm.

3. Chip Heath and Dan Heath, Switch: *How to Change Things When Change Is Hard* (New York: Crown Business, 2010).

4. Lillian Cunningham, "In big move, Accenture will get rid of performance reviews and rankings," *Washington Post,* July 21, 2015, http://www.washingtonpost.com/news/on-leadership/wp/2015/07/21/in-big-move-accenture-will-get-rid-of-annual-performance-reviews-and-rankings/.

5. John P. Kotter and Dan S. Cohen, *The Heart of Change: Real-Life Stories of How People Change Their Organizations* (Boston, MA: Harvard Business Review Press, 2012), 37.

6. Heath and Heath, *Switch.*

7. Seth Godin, "A Bird in Search of a Cage," Seth's Blog, February 5, 2015, http://sethgodin.typepad.com/seths_blog/2015/02/a-bird-in-search-of-a-cage.html.

8. Rosabeth Moss Kanter, "Ten Reasons People Resist Change," *Harvard Business Review,* September 25, 2012, accessed February 18, 2015, http://blogs.hbr.org/2012/09/ten-reasons-people-resist-chang/.

9. 9. Merriam-Webster Dictionary, s.v. "courage," accessed February 28, 2015, http://www.merriam-webster.com/dictionary/courage.

10. Rosalynn Carter, Biography.com, http://www.biography.com/people/rosalynn-carter-9240052#road-to-the-white-house.

Final Thoughts

1. Shawn Parr, "Culture Eats Strategy for Lunch," *Fast Company,* January 24, 2012, accessed February 25, 2015, http://www.fastcompany.com/1810674/culture-eats-strategy-lunch.

2. Seth Godin, *Poke the Box* (Steamboat Springs, CO: Portfolio, 2015).

References

Articles

Ariely, Dan. "What's the Value of a Big Bonus?" *New York Times,* November 19, 2008. Accessed February 28, 2015. http://www.nytimes.com/2008/11/20/opinion/20ariely.html?_r=0.

Associated Press. "US Economy May Be Stuck in Slow Lane for Long Run." CNBC, February 10, 2014. http://www.cnbc.com/id/101402528.

Banner, D. K., and R. A. Cooke. "Ethical Dilemmas in Performance Appraisal." *Journal of Business Ethics* 3, issue 4 (1984): 327–33.

Bennett, Nathan, and G. James Lemoine. "What VUCA Really Means for You." *Harvard Business Review,* January–February 2014. Accessed February 8, 2015. https://hbr.org/2014/01/what-vuca-really-means-for-you/ar/1.

Bersin, Josh. "The Myth of the Bell Curve: Look for the Hyper-Performers." *Forbes,* February 9, 2014. Accessed February 8, 2015. http://www.forbes.com/sites/joshbersin/2014/02/19/the-myth-of-the-bell-curve-look-for-the-hyper-performers/.

Bock, Diane. "Performance Management: The Final Frontier?" Development Dimensions International, September 2014. Accessed February 8, 2015. http://www.ddiworld.com/blog/tmi/september-2014/performance-management-the-final-frontier#.VNa2PfnF_Ro.

Buckingham, Marcus. "Most HR Data Is Bad Data." *Harvard Business Review,* February 9, 2015. https://hbr.org/2015/02/most-hr-data-is-bad-data.

———. "Putting the Strengths-Based Perspective to Work." The Marcus Buckingham Company (TMBC), 2010: 2. Accessed February 8, 2015. http://www.tmbc.com/legacy/sites/default/files/services_downloads/Strengths_White_Paper.pdf.

Burg, Natalie. "How Technology Has Changed Workplace Communication." *Forbes,* December 20, 2013. Accessed February 8, 2015. http://www.forbes.com/sites/unify/2013/12/10/how-technology-has-changed-workplace-communication/.

Cappelli, Peter. "Should Performance Reviews Be Fired?" Wharton Center for Human Resources, April 27, 2011, accessed February 8, 2015. http://knowledge.wharton.upenn.edu/article/should-performance-reviews-be-fired/.

CEB. *Breakthrough Performance in the New Work Environment: Identifying and Enabling the New High Performer.* http://www.executiveboard.com/exbd-resources/pdf/executive-guidance/eg2013-annual-final.pdf.

Chamorro-Premuzic, Tomas. "Does Money Really Affect Motivation? A Review of the Research." *Harvard Business Review,* April 2013. Accessed February 8, 2015. https://hbr.org/2013/04/does-money-really-affect-motiv/.

Cohn, Emily. "The Job Market Is Still Years Away from a Full Recovery." *Huffington Post,* January 11, 2015. Accessed February 8, 2015. http://www.huffingtonpost.com/ 2015/01/11/job-market-recovery-years-away_n_6451810.html.

CRG emPerform. "Does Your Performance Rating Scale Need Improvement?" *Employee Performance & Talent Management,* May 6, 2014. Accessed February 8, 2015. http://www.employee-performance.com/blog/does-your-performance-rating-scale-need-improvement/.

Cunningham, Lillian. "In Big Move, Accenture Will Get Rid of Performance Reviews and Rankings." *Washington Post,* July 21, 2015. http://www.washingtonpost.com/ news/on-leadership/wp/2015/07/21/in-big-move-accenture-will-get-rid-of-annual-performance-reviews-and-rankings/.

Deci, Edward L. "Intrinsic Motivation, Extrinsic Reinforcement, and Inequity." *Journal of Personality and Social Psychology* 22, no. 1 (March 1972): 119–20. http://www.researchgate.net/publication/232461387_Intrinsic_motivation_ extrinsic_reinforcement_and_inequity.

Dewhurst, Martin, Matthew Guthridge, and Elizabeth Mohr. "Motivating people: Getting Beyond Money." *McKinsey Quarterly,* November 2009. Accessed February 8, 2015. http://www.mckinsey.com/insights/organization/ motivating_people_getting_beyond_money.

Drucker, P. F. "Managing Oneself." *Harvard Business Review,* January 2005. Accessed September 4, 2015. https://hbr.org/2005/01/managing-oneself.

Dubay, Curtis S., and Stephen Moore. *Economy Better, but Still Growing Too Slowly Because of Anti-Growth Policy.* Heritage Foundation. Issue Brief #4144. February 6, 2014. Accessed February 8, 2015. http://www.heritage.org/research/ reports/2014/02/us-economy-growing-slowly-because-of-anti-growth-policy.

DuBois-Maahs, Jessica. "Should Salaries Be Transparent?" *Talent Management,* December 12, 2013. Accessed February 8, 2015. http://www.talentmgt.com/ articles/should-salaries-be-transparent.

Falvey, Becky, and Lauren Ammon. "6 Tips for Better Performance Reviews." *Resource Center and Industry Insights,* February 10, 2014. Webinar and article. http://www.paycor.com/resource-center/6-tips-for-better-performance-reviews.

Gilbert, Jay. "The Millennials: A New Generation of Employees, a New Set of Engagement Policies." *Ivey Business Journal,* September/October 2011. http://iveybusinessjournal.com/topics/the-workplace/the-millennials-a-new-generation-of-employees-a-new-set-of-engagement-policies#.VMF_TSvF_Rp.

Globoforce. "Executive Brief: Performance Management, Meet the Wisdom of Crowds." 2012. http://talentsnapshot.com/wp-content/uploads/2012/11/Performance-Mgmt-Meet-the-Wisdom-of-Crowds.pdf.

———. "The Science of Happiness: How to Build a Killer Culture in Your Company." 2013. http://go.globoforce.com/ppc-rem-science-happiness-2014.html.

Gould, Elise. "At an Average of 246,000 Jobs a Month in 2014, It Will Be the Summer of 2017 Before We Return to Pre-recession Labor Market Health." Working Economics Blog, Economic Policy Institute, January 9, 2015. http://www.epi.org/blog/at-an-average-of-246000-jobs-a-month-in-2014-it-will-be-the-summer-of-2017-before-we-return-to-pre-recession-labor-market-health/.

Gupta, Nina, and Atul Mitra. "The Value of Financial Incentives: Myths and Empirical Realities." *ACA Journal* 7, no. 3 (Autumn 1998): 62.

Hamel, Gary. "First, Let's Fire All the Managers." *Harvard Business Review,* December 2011. https://hbr.org/2011/12/first-lets-fire-all-the-managers/ar/1.
———. "Moon Shots for Management." *Harvard Business Review,* February 2009. https://hbr.org/2009/02/moon-shots-for-management.

Harvard Business Press. *Harvard Business Essentials: Performance Management: Measure and Improve the Effectiveness of Your Employees.* Boston: Harvard Business School Press, June 1, 2006.

Irwin, Neil. "Why It Doesn't Feel Like a Recovery." *Washington Post.* Accessed February 8, 2015. http://www.washingtonpost.com/wp-srv/business/the-output-gap/.

Jacobsen, Darcy. "The Exceedingly Curious Origins of Performance Management." Globoforce. March 20, 2013. Accessed February 8, 2015. http://www.globoforce.com/gfblog/2013/the-exceedingly-curious-origins-of-performance-management.

Johnson, Bradford C., James M. Maniyika, and Lareina A. Yee. "The Next Revolution in Interactions." *McKinsey Quarterly,* November 2005: 25–26. http://www.mckinsey.com/insights/organization/the_next_revolution_in_interactions.

Lawrence, Kirk. "Developing Leaders in a VUCA Environment." UNC Kenan-Flagler Business School. 2013. http://www.growbold.com/2013/developing-leaders-in-a-vuca-environment_UNC.2013.pdf.

London School of Economics and Political Science. "When Performance-Related Pay Backfires." June 25, 2009. http://www.lse.ac.uk/newsAndMedia/news/archives/2009/06/performancepay.aspx.

Meister, Jeanne. "Corporate Social Responsibility: A Lever for Employee Attraction & Engagement." *Forbes,* June 7, 2012. http://www.forbes.com/sites/jeannemeister/2012/06/07/corporate-social-responsibility-a-lever-for-employee-attraction-engagement/.

Miller, Beth. "Banish 'Annual' from Your Performance Review Vocabulary." *Entrepreneur,* October 10, 2014. http://www.entrepreneur.com/article/237585.

Morrison, Carol. "How to Align Your Employees to Strategic and Business Goals." *i4CP Productivity Blog,* October 31, 2014. http://www.i4cp.com/productivity-blog/2014/10/31/how-to-align-your-employees-to-strategic-and-business-goals.

Mosley, Eric. "Performance Management Meets the Wisdom of Crowds." Globoforce, 2012. Accessed February 8, 2015 http://www.engagementstrategiesonline.com/Performance-Management-Meets-the-Wisdom-of-Crowds/.

Moss Kanter, Rosabeth. "Ten Reasons People Resist Change." *Harvard Business Review,* September 25, 2012. https://hbr.org/2012/09/ten-reasons-people-resist-chang/.

Murphy, Mark. "The 3 Reasons Employees Hate Performance Reviews." *Leadership IQ,* May 1, 2012. http://www.hr.com/en/app/blog/2012/05/leadership-iq-article--the-3-reasons-employees-hat_h1p3ce7e.html.

Noguchi, Yuki. "Behold the Entrenched—and Reviled—Annual Review." NPR, October 28, 2014. http://www.npr.org/2014/10/28/358636126/behold-the-entrenched-and-reviled-annual-review.

Ordóñez, Lisa D., et al. "Goals Gone Wild: The Systematic Side Effects of Over-Prescribing Goal Setting." Harvard Business School Working Paper 09-083, February 2009. http://www.hbs.edu/faculty/Publication%20Files/09-083.pdf.

Rao, Venkatesh. "An Organization Design Renaissance." *Forbes,* May 2012. http://www.forbes.com/sites/venkateshrao/2012/05/07/an-organization-design-renaissance/.

Reeves, Martin, Claire Love, and Nishant Mathur. "The Most Adaptive Companies 2012: Winning in an Age of Turbulence." *BCG Perspectives,* August 21, 2012. https://www.bcgperspectives.com/content/articles/corporate_strategy_portfolio_management_future_of_strategy_most_adaptive_companies_2012/#chapter1.

Resker, Jamie. "Performance Feedback Training for Managers." *Managing Employee Performance Blog,* September 29, 2013. http://info.employeeperformancesolutions.com/managing-employee-performance-blog/ bid/87164/Performance-Feedback-Training-for-Managers.

Rock, David, Josh Davis, and Beth Jones. "Kill Your Performance Ratings: Neuroscience Shows Why Numbers-Based HR Management Is Obsolete." *Strategy+Business,* issue 76 (Autumn 2014). http://www.strategy-business.com/media/file/00275_Kill_Your_Perfomance_Ratings.pdf.

Schawbel, Dan. "Groundbreaking Survey Reveals the Rise of Freedom-Seeking Freelancers and Redefinition of Entrepreneurship." Millennial Branding, May 14, 2013. http://millennialbranding.com/2013/millennials-future-work-study/.

Schwartz, Tony. "The Only Thing That Really Matters." *Harvard Business Review,* June 1, 2011. https://hbr.org/2011/06/the-only-thing-that-really-mat.html.

Slocum, David. "Six Creative Leadership Lessons from the Military in an Era of VUCA and COIN." *Forbes,* October 8, 2013. http://www.forbes.com/sites/berlinschoolofcreativeleadership/ 2013/10/08/six-creative-leadership-lessons-from-the-military-in-an-era-of-vuca-and-coin/.

Smith, John. "The Traditional Rating Scale: Needs Improvement." *Employee Performance & Talent Management,* February 22, 2011. http://www.employee-performance.com/blog/the-traditional-rating-scale-needs-improvement/.

Stevenson, Cliff. "Performance Management: Sticking With What Doesn't Work." *i4cp TrendWatcher,* Issue 583, October 31, 2013. http://www.i4cp.com/trendwatchers/2013/10/31/performance-management-sticking-with-what-doesn-t-work.

Sullivan, John. "How the Talent Management Function Can Thrive in a VUCA World." *Talent Management Intelligence,* Development Dimensions International (DDI), 2013. Accessed February 8, 2015. http://blogs.ddiworld.com/tmi/2013/10/how-the-talent-management-function-can-thrive-in-a-vuca-world.html.

Trakstar. "3 Steps to Flatten Rater Bias." September 12, 2013. http://www.trakstar.com/blog-post/3-steps-to-flatten-rater-bias/.

Vara, Vauhini. "The Push Against Performance Reviews." *New Yorker,* July 24, 2015. http://www.newyorker.com/business/currency/the-push-against-performance-reviews.

Vorhauser-Smith, Sylvia. "How the Best Places to Work Are Nailing Employee Engagement." *Forbes,* August 2013. http://www.forbes.com/sites/sylviavorhausersmith/2013/08/14/how-the-best-places-to-work-are-nailing-employee-engagement/.

————. "Three Reasons Performance Management Will Change in 2013." *Forbes.* December 16, 2012. http://www.forbes.com/sites/sylviavorhausersmith/2012/12/16/the-new-face-of-performance-management-trading-annual-reviews-for-agile-management/2/.

The Week staff. "How Millennials Are Transforming the Workplace." *The Week,* August 24, 2012. Accessed February 8, 2015. http://theweek.com/articles/472913/millennials-are-transforming-workplace.

Williams, Ray. "Like It or Not, Millennials Will Change the Workplace." *Financial Post,* September 16, 2013. http://business. financialpost.com/2013/09/16/like-it-or-not-millennials-will-change-the-workplace/.

————. "Why CEOs Need to Scrap Employee Performance Reviews." *Psychology Today,* May 17, 2011. http://www.psychologytoday.com/blog/wired-success/201105/why-ceos-need-scrap-employee-performance-reviews.

Wirthman, Lisa. "Is Flat Better? Zappos Ditches Hierarchy to Improve Company Performance." *Forbes,* January 7, 2014. http://www.forbes.com/sites/sungardas/2014/01/07/is-flat-better-zappos-ditches-hierarchy-to-improve-company-performance/.

Wong, Yishan. "The Peculiar Origins of the Performance Review, and Other HR Bureaucracy." *Forbes,* February 11, 2012. http://www.forbes.com/sites/yishanwong/2012/02/11/the-peculiar-origins-of-the-performance-review-and-other-hr-bureaucracy/.

Zenger, Jack, Joe Folkman, and Scott Edinger. "How Extraordinary Leaders Double Profits." Chief Learning Officer. June 28, 2009. http://www.clomedia.com/articles/how_extraordinary_leaders_double_profits.

Studies

Deci, Edward L., Richard M. Ryan, and Richard Koestner. "A Meta-Analytic Review of Experiments Examining the Effects of Extrinsic Rewards on Intrinsic Motivation." *Psychological Bulletin* 125, issue 6 (1999), 659.

Ernst and Young. "Building a Better Working World." PRNewswire, September 3, 2013. http://www.multivu.com/mnr/63068-ernst-and-young-llp-research-younger-managers-rise-in-the-ranks.

————. *Younger Managers Rise in the Ranks: An Ernest and Young Study on Generational Shifts in the US Workplace.* June 2013. http://www.ey.com/US/en/Issues/Talent-management/Talent-Survey-The-generational-management-shift.

Gensler. *2013 US Workplace Survey.* July 15, 2013. http://www.gensler.com/uploads/documents/2013_US_Workplace_Survey_07_15_2013.pdf.

i4CP. *The 2006 Performance Management Survey.* November 30, 2006. http://www.i4cp.com/news/2006/11/30/the-2006-performance-management-survey.

Reeves, Martin, Claire Love, and Nishant Mathur. "The Most Adaptive Companies 2012: Winning in an Age of Turbulence." *BCG Perspectives.* Boston Consulting Group, August 21, 2012. Accessed February 8, 2015. https://www.bcgperspectives.com/content/articles/corporate_strategy_portfolio_management_future_of_strategy_most_adaptive_companies_2012/#chapter1.

Rock, David, Josh Davis, and Beth Jones. "Kill Your Performance Ratings." *Strategy and Business,* Autumn 2014. http://digitaledition.strategy-business.com/article/Kill+Your+Performance+Ratings/ 1775896/219771/article.html.

Schawbel, Dan. "Millennial Branding and Beyond.com Survey Reveals the Rising Cost of Hiring Workers from the Millennial Generation," August 6, 2013. http://millennialbranding.com/2013/cost-millennial-retention-study/.

Society for Human Resource Management. *SHRM Workplace Forecast: The Top Workplace Trends According to HR Professionals.* May 2013. http://www.shrm.org/Research/FutureWorkplaceTrends/Documents/13-0146%20Workplace_Forecast_FULL_FNL.pdf.

US Department of Commerce, Bureau of Economic Analysis. National Income and Products Accounts. Gross Domestic Product and Corporate Profits: Second Quarter 2015. August 27, 2015. http://www.bea.gov/newsreleases/national/gdp/gdpnewsrelease.htm.

Whiting, Dr. Jim, Elizabeth Jones, Dr. David Rock, and Xenia Bendit. "Lead change with the brain in mind." *NeuroLeadership Journal,* issue 4. Accessed February 8, 2015. http://www.davidrock.net/files/07_Lead_change_with_the_brain_in_mind_US.pdf.

WorldatWork and Sibson Consulting. 2010 *Study on the State of Performance Management.* Sibson Consulting. October 2010. Accessed February 8, 2015. http://www.worldatwork.org/waw/adimLink?id=44473.

Presentations

Bohannon, Scott. "Confronting Six Enemies of Post-Recession Performance." Webinar by Corporate Executive Board (CEB). October 14, 2010.

CEB. *Driving Breakthrough Performance in the New Work Environment: Identifying and Enabling the New High Performer.* 2012. Accessed February 8, 2015. http://www.executiveboard.com/exbd-resources/pdf/executive-guidance/eg2013-annual-final.pdf.

Cornerstone. *Reimagine Work.* 2014. http://www.cornerstoneondemand.com/sites/default/files/insight/csod-in-reimagine-work.pdf.

Deloitte. *The Connected Workplace: War for talent in the digital economy.* 2013. http://www2.deloitte.com/au/en/pages/economics/articles/the-connected-workplace.html.

Hauer, Terry, and Stacia Sherman Garr. "How Kelly Services Abandoned the Performance Score: Part 2 of the Abolishing Performance Scores Webinar Series." Bersin, October 2013. http://www.bersin.com/News/EventDetails.aspx?id=16775.

Levensaler, Leighanne. *The Essential Guide to Employee Performance Management Practices: Part 1.* Bersin, October 15, 2008. http://www.bersin.com/Store/Details.aspx?docid=10337744.

McKinsey & Company. "Leaders everywhere: A conversation with Gary Hamel." May 2013. http://www.mckinsey.com/insights/organization/leaders_everywhere_a_conversation_with_gary_hamel.

Books

Adams, J. Stacey, Jerald Greenberg, and Robert A. Baron. *Behavior in Organizations.* 5th ed. Englewood Cliffs, NJ: Prentice Hall, 1995.

Anchor, Shawn. *The Happiness Advantage: The Seven Principles of Positive Psychology That Fuel Success and Performance at Work.* New York: Crown Business, 2010.

Axelrod, Wendy, and Jeannie Coyle. *Make Talent Your Business: How Exceptional Managers Develop People While Getting Results.* San Francisco: Berrett-Koehler Publishers, 2011.

Bellman, Geoffrey, and Kathleen Ryan. *Extraordinary Groups: How Ordinary Teams Achieve Amazing Results.* San Francisco: Jossey-Bass, 2009.

Bennett, Sam, and Keegan-Michael Key. *Get It Done: From Procrastination to Creative Genius in 15 Minutes a Day.* Novato, CA: New World Library, 2014.

Berger, Lance, and Dorothy Berger. *The Talent Management Handbook: Creating a Sustainable Competitive Advantage by Selecting, Developing, and Promoting the Best People.* New York: McGraw-Hill Professional Publishing, 2010.

Block, Peter. *Flawless Consulting: A Guide to Getting Your Expertise Used.* 3rd ed. San Francisco: Pfeiffer, 2011.

———. *Stewardship: Choosing Service Over Self-Interest.* San Francisco: Berrett-Koehler Publishers, 1993.

Buckingham, Marcus. *Go Put Your Strengths to Work: 6 Powerful Steps to Achieve Outstanding Performance.* New York: Free Press, 2010.

———. *StandOut: The Groundbreaking New Strengths Assessment from the Leader of the Strengths Revolution.* Nashville, TN: Thomas Nelson, 2011.

Buckingham, Marcus, and Donald O. Clifton. *Now, Discover Your Strengths.* New York: Free Press, 2001.

Caraher, Lee. *Millennials & Management: The Essential Guide to Making It Work at Work.* Brookline, MA: Bibliomotion Inc., 2015.

Clark, Boyd, and Ron Crossland. *The Leader's Voice: How Your Communication Can Inspire Action and Get Results!* New York: Select Books, 2002.

Coens, Tom, and Mary Jenkins. *Abolishing Performance Appraisals: Why They Backfire and What to Do Instead.* San Francisco: Berrett-Koehler Publishers, 2002.

Cohen, Allan R., and David L. Bradford. *Influence Without Authority.* 2nd ed. Hoboken, NJ: Wiley, 2005.

Collins, Jim. *How the Mighty Fall: And Why Some Companies Never Give In.* New York: Jim Collins, 2009.

Covey, Stephen R. *Principle-Centered Leadership.* New York: Simon & Schuster, 1992.

Crane, Thomas G., and Lerissa Nancy Patrick. *The Heart of Coaching: Using Transformational Coaching to Create a High-Performance Coaching Culture.* New York: F T A Press, 2012.

Culbert, Samuel A., and Lawrence Rout. *Get Rid of the Performance Review!: How Companies Can Stop Intimidating, Start Managing—and Focus on What Really Matters.* New York: Business Plus, 2010.

Daniels, Aubrey C. *OOPS! 13 Management Practices That Waste Time & Money (and what to do instead).* Atlanta, GA: Performance Management Publications, 2009.

Deci, Edward L. *Why We Do What We Do: Understanding Self-Motivation.* New York: Penguin, 1995.

Deming, W. Edwards. *Out of the Crisis.* Reprint ed. Cambridge, MA: MIT Press, 2000.

Dykstra, Josh Allan. *Igniting the Invisible Tribe: Designing an Organization That Doesn't Suck.* Pismo Beach, CA: Silver Thread Publishing. 2012.

Fried, Jason, and David Heinemeier Hansson. *Rework.* New York: Crown Business, 2010.

Fullan, Michael. *Change Leader: Learning to Do What Matters Most.* San Francisco: Jossey-Bass, 2011.

Fulton, Roger. *Common Sense Leadership: A Handbook for Success as a Leader.* New York: Barnes & Noble Books, 2001.

Garvin, David A. *Learning in Action: A Guide to Putting the Learning Organization to Work.* Boston, MA: Harvard Business Review Press, 2003.

George, C. S., Jr. *The History of Management Thought.* Englewood Cliffs, NJ: Prentice-Hall, Inc., 1972.

Godin, Seth. *The Big Moo: Stop Trying to Be Perfect and Start Being Remarkable.* New York: Portfolio, 2005.

———. *The Icarus Deception: How High Will You Fly?* New York: Portfolio, 2012.

———. *Poke the Box: When Was the Last Time You Did Something for the First Time?* New York: Portfolio, 2011.

———. *Purple Cow: Transform Your Business by Being Remarkable.* New York: Portfolio, 2009.

———. *Small Is the New Big: And 183 Other Riffs, Rants, and Remarkable Business Ideas.* New York: Portfolio, 2006.

———. *Tribes: We Need You to Lead Us.* New York: Portfolio, 2008.

———. *V Is for Vulnerable: Life Outside the Comfort Zone.* New York: Portfolio, 2012.

Goldsmith, Marshall, and Mark Reiter. *What Got You Here Won't Get You There: How Successful People Become Even More Successful.* New York: Hachette Books, 2007.

Goleman, Daniel. *Emotional Intelligence: Why It Can Matter More Than IQ.* New York: Bantam Books, 2005.

Hamel, Gary. *The Future of Management.* Boston, MA: Harvard Business Review Press, 2007.

———. *What Matters Now: How to Win in a World of Relentless Change, Ferocious Competition, and Unstoppable Innovation.* San Francisco: Jossey-Bass, 2012.

Hammer, Michael, and James Champy. *Reengineering the Corporation: A Manifesto for Business Revolution.* New York: HarperBusiness, 2006.

Harkins, Phil. *Powerful Conversations: How High Impact Leaders Communicate.* New York: McGraw-Hill Education, 1999.

Harmon, Roy L., and Leroy D. Peterson. *Reinventing the Factory: Productivity Breakthroughs in Manufacturing Today,* Vol. 1. New York: Free Press, 1989.

Harvey Yao, Sara. *Get Present: Simple Strategies to Get Out of Your Head and Lead More Powerfully.* Elements of Power, 2013.

Heath, Chip, and Dan Heath. *Switch: How to Change Things When Change Is Hard.* New York: Crown Business, 2010.

Hickman, Craig, and Tom Smith. *The Oz Principle: Getting Results Through Individual and Organizational Accountability.* New York: Portfolio, 2010.

Holman, Peggy, and Tom Devane. *The Change Handbook: The Definitive Resource on Today's Best Methods for Engaging Whole Systems.* San Francisco: Berrett-Koehler Publishers, 2007.

Hope, Jeremy, and Steve Player. *Beyond Performance Management: Why, When, and How to Use 40 Tools and Best Practices for Superior Business Performance.* Boston, MA: Harvard Business Review, 2012.

Johansen, Bob, and John R. Ryan. *Leaders Make the Future: Ten New Leadership Skills for an Uncertain World.* San Francisco: Berrett-Koehler Publishers, 2012.

Johnson, H. Thomas, and Andres Broms. *Profit Beyond Measure—Extraordinary Results Through Attention to Work and People.* New York: Free Press, 2000.

Kawasaki, Guy. *Enchantment: The Art of Changing Hearts, Minds, and Actions.* New York: Portfolio, 2011.

Kaye, Beverly, and Sharon Jordan-Evans. *Love 'Em or Lose 'Em: Getting Good People to Stay.* San Francisco: Berrett-Koehler Publishers, 2014.

Kohn, Alfie. *Punished by Rewards: The Trouble with Gold Stars, Incentive Plans, A's, Praise, and Other Bribes.* New York: Mariner Books, 1999.

Kotter, John P. *Leading Change.* Boston MA: Harvard Business Review Press, 2012.

Koulopoulos, Thomas, and Dan Keldsen. *The Gen Z Effect: The Six Forces Shaping the Future of Business.* Brookline, MA: Bibliomotion, 2014.

Maister, David H. *Managing the Professional Service Firm.* New York: Free Press, 1997.

Manganelli, Raymond L., and Mark M. Klein. *The Reengineering Handbook: A Step-by-Step Guide to Business Transformation.* New York: AMACOM, 1994.

Markle, Garold L. *Catalytic Coaching: The End of the Performance Review.* Westport, CT: Praeger Publishing, 2000.

Maurer, Rick. *Feedback Toolkit: 16 Tools for Better Communication in the Workplace.* Portland, OR: Productivity Press, 1994.

———. *Feedback Toolkit: 16 Tools for Better Communication in the Workplace,* Second Edition. Portland, OR: Productivity Press, 2011.

Maxwell, John C. *How Successful People Think: Change Your Thinking, Change Your Life.* New York: Center Street of Hachette Book Group, 2009.

Maxwell, John C., and Stephen R. Covey. *The 21 Irrefutable Laws of Leadership: Follow Them and People Will Follow You.* Nashville, TN: Thomas Nelson, 2007.

Mintzberg, Henry. *Managers Not MBAs: A Hard Look at the Soft Practice of Managing and Management Development.* San Francisco: Berrett-Koehler Publishers, 2005.

Mosley, Eric. *The Crowdsourced Performance Review: How to Use the Power of Social Recognition to Transform Employee Performance.* New York: McGraw-Hill, 2013.

Oakes, Kevin, and Pat Galagan. *The Executive Guide to Integrated Talent Management.* Alexandria, VA: ASTD, 2011.

Oshry, Barry. *Leading Systems: Lessons from the Power Lab.* San Francisco: Berrett-Koehler Publishers, 1999.

Petrozzo, Daniel P., and John C. Stepper. *Successful Reengineering.* Hoboken, NJ: Wiley, 1994.

Pink, Daniel H. *Drive: The Surprising Truth About What Motivates Us.* New York: Riverhead Books, 2011.

Pollock, Roy V. H., Andrew McK. Jefferson, and Calhoun W. Wick. *The Six Disciplines of Breakthrough Learning: How to Turn Training and Development into Business Results.* New York: Pfeiffer, 2010.

Pulakos, Elaine D. *Performance Management: A New Approach for Driving Business Results.* New Jersey: Blackwell Publishing, 2009.

Reeve, Jonmarshall. *Understanding Motivation and Emotion.* 4th ed. Hoboken, NJ: Wiley, 2005.

Renvoise, Patrick, and Christophe Morin. *Neuromarketing: Understanding the Buy Buttons in Your Customer's Brain.* Nashville, TN: Thomas Nelson, 2007.

Ressler, Cali, and Jody Thompson. *Why Work Sucks and How to Fix It: The Results-Only Revolution.* New York: Penguin, 2010.

Richards, Dick. *Artful Work: Awakening Joy, Meaning, and Commitment in the Workplace.* San Francisco: Berrett-Koehler Publishers, 1995.

Rock, David. *Your Brain at Work: Strategies for Overcoming Distraction, Regaining Focus, and Working Smarter All Day Long.* New York: HarperBusiness, 2009.

Rosenzweig, Phil. *The Halo Effect: . . . and the Eight Other Business Delusions That Deceive Managers.* New York: Free Press, 2014.

Rummler, Geary A., and Alan P. Brache. *Improving Performance: How to Manage the White Space on the Organization Chart.* San Francisco: Jossey-Bass, 2012.

Russell, Jeff. *Do What You Do Best: Outsourcing as Capacity Building in the Nonprofit Sector.* Boise, ID: Elevate, 2013.

Ryan, M. J. *AdaptAbility: How to Survive Change You Didn't Ask For. Your Coach In A Box,* 2009.

Scholtes, Peter R. *The Leader's Handbook.* New York: McGraw-Hill, 1998 (chapter 9).

Schwartz, Peter. *The Art of the Long View: Planning for the Future in an Uncertain World.* New York: Doubleday, 1996.

Scott, Susan. *Fierce Conversations: Achieving Success at Work and in Life, One Conversation at a Time.* New York: Berkley Books, 2004.

———. *Fierce Leadership: A Bold Alternative to the Worst "Best" Practices of Business Today.* New York: Crown Business, 2011.

Scott, W. D., R. C. Clothier, and W. R. Spriegel. *Personnel Management.* New York: McGraw-Hill, 1941.

Senge, Peter. *The Fifth Discipline.* New York: Doubleday, 1990.

———. *The Fifth Discipline: The Art & Practice of the Learning Organization.* New York: Doubleday, 2006.

Shaw, Haydn. *Sticking Points: How to Get 4 Generations Working Together in the 12 Places They Come Apart.* Carol Stream, IL: Tyndale House Publishers, Inc., 2013.

Smither, James W. *Performance Appraisal: State of the Art in Practice.* San Francisco: Jossey-Bass, 1998.

Spitzer, Dean R. *Transforming Performance Measurement: Rethinking the Way We Measure and Drive Organizational Success.* New York: AMACOM, 2007.

Tichy, Noel M., and Warren G. Bennis. *Judgment: How Winning Leaders Make Great Calls.* New York: Portfolio, 2009.

Waller, Graham, and Karen Rubenstrunk. *The CIO Edge: Seven Leadership Skills You Need to Drive Results.* Boston MA: Harvard Business Review Press, 2010.

Wheatley, Margaret J. *Leadership and the New Science.* San Francisco: Berrett-Koehler Publishers, 1992.

Wheatley, Margaret J., and Myron Kellner-Rogers. *A Simpler Way.* San Francisco: Berrett-Koehler Publishers, 1996.

Young, Stephen. *Micromessaging: Why Great Leadership Is Beyond Words.* New York: McGraw-Hill, 2006.

TED Talks

Fried, Jason. "Why work doesn't happen at work." TED Talk, October 2010. http://www.ted.com/talks/jason_fried_why_work_doesn_t_happen_at_work?language=en.

Pink, Daniel. "The puzzle of motivation." TED Talk, July 2009. http://www.ted.com/talks/dan_pink_on_motivation.html.

Robbins, Tony. "Why we do what we do." TED Talk, February 2006. http://www.ted.com/talks/tony_robbins_asks_why_we_do_what_we_do?language=en.

Sinek, Simon. "How great leaders inspire action." TED Talk, September 2009. http://www.ted.com/talks/simon_sinek_how_great_leaders_inspire_action?language=en.

Talgam, Itay. "Lead like the great conductors." TED Talk, October 2009. https://www.ted.com/talks/itay_talgam_lead_like_the_great_conductors/transcript?language=en.

Acknowledgments

THANKS TO:

Jenni Clark, who has been on this journey with me from the beginning: Jenni, I'm so fortunate to have you in my sidecar; Katie Henry, whose razor-sharp contributions, unique ability to keep us moving forward, and marketing savvy have been invaluable to this project; and my dear husband, Jeff Mosier: Your editing support not only turned the good into great but also has reinforced the power of our partnership. I'm grateful to all three of you for riding along with me, as we negotiated the many blind curves and celebrated the milestones along the way. I think we make one powerful team.

My brilliant editor, Neal Maillet, for fielding my SOS call and taking a chance on this new writer, and to the full Berrett-Koehler team for their warm welcome to the BK family.

Dave Ulrich, for your thoughtful and insightful foreword. I am honored and deeply grateful.

Jeannie Coyle, who has influenced me all along the way with her generosity, early advice, and insightful review, as well as Karen Hornin and Sara Jane Hope, for their detailed and astute reviews of my manuscript.

Terri Fincham-Conner, for her added levity, honest reviews, and heartfelt support along the way.

Geoff Bellman, for the advice and connections that were the seeds of so much.

The Tribe at PeopleFirm, for their support, encouragement, and cheers throughout the process. A special call-out to Sam Crumley, Laura Denning, Scott Perkins, Sara Gaccione, and Bill Hefferman for your early reviews and ongoing support over the many months.

The many clients who have allowed me to learn and grow throughout my career.

My parents, for instilling in me their entrepreneurial spirit, for always believing I could do anything, and for caring for our little family when I was most immersed in this project.

My kids, Ivy and Wilson, for always making me laugh and helping me remember what really matters.

And finally to Perry, Luna Fox, and Edina, for keeping me company throughout the long hours of writing. Thanks in particular to Ed for her determined barking when it really was time to call it a night.

Index

About the Author

M. TAMRA CHANDLER IS A BONA FIDE PEOPLE MAVEN. What is that, you ask? It's someone who's spent the majority of her career thinking about people, researching how they're motivated, and developing new and effective ways for organizations to achieve the ultimate win-win: inspired people driving inspiring performance. She's also the CEO and cofounder of a thriving Seattle-based consulting company called PeopleFirm, which focuses on helping organizations find success by improving how they utilize, motivate, and support—you guessed it—their people.

An award-winning leader in her field (she's been recognized by *Consulting Magazine* twice as one of the top consultants in the United States), Tamra has more than twenty-five years of experience guiding clients ranging from tiny nonprofit arts groups to giant multinational corporations through varied and complex business transformation projects. She's recently focused her considerable energy on solving the problem of performance management. Her Performance Management Reboot system has received international acclaim for its innovative, customizable, and down-to-earth methodology. It stands out in a field that's awash in criticism but sorely lacking in real answers.

Outside her work, Tamra treasures any free time she can find with her husband, two children, and three pedigreed mutts.

Berrett–Koehler
Publishers

Berrett-Koehler is an independent publisher dedicated to an ambitious mission: *connecting people and ideas to create a world that works for all*.

We believe that to truly create a better world, action is needed at all levels—individual, organizational, and societal. At the individual level, our publications help people align their lives with their values and with their aspirations for a better world. At the organizational level, our publications promote progressive leadership and management practices, socially responsible approaches to business, and humane and effective organizations. At the societal level, our publications advance social and economic justice, shared prosperity, sustainability, and new solutions to national and global issues.

A major theme of our publications is "Opening Up New Space." Berrett-Koehler titles challenge conventional thinking, introduce new ideas, and foster positive change. Their common quest is changing the underlying beliefs, mindsets, institutions, and structures that keep generating the same cycles of problems, no matter who our leaders are or what improvement programs we adopt.

We strive to practice what we preach—to operate our publishing company in line with the ideas in our books. At the core of our approach is stewardship, which we define as a deep sense of responsibility to administer the company for the benefit of all of our "stakeholder" groups: authors, customers, employees, investors, service providers, and the communities and environment around us.

We are grateful to the thousands of readers, authors, and other friends of the company who consider themselves to be part of the "BK Community." We hope that you, too, will join us in our mission.

A BK Business Book

This book is part of our BK Business series. BK Business titles pioneer new and progressive leadership and management practices in all types of public, private, and nonprofit organizations. They promote socially responsible approaches to business, innovative organizational change methods, and more humane and effective organizations.

Berrett–Koehler
Publishers

Connecting people and ideas
to create a world that works for all

Dear Reader,

Thank you for picking up this book and joining our worldwide community of Berrett-Koehler readers. We share ideas that bring positive change into people's lives, organizations, and society.

To welcome you, we'd like to offer you a free e-book. You can pick from among twelve of our bestselling books by entering the promotional code **BKP92E** here: http://www.bkconnection.com/welcome.

When you claim your free e-book, we'll also send you a copy of our e-news-letter, the *BK Communiqué*. Although you're free to unsubscribe, there are many benefits to sticking around. In every issue of our newsletter you'll find

- A free e-book
- Tips from famous authors
- Discounts on spotlight titles
- Hilarious insider publishing news
- A chance to win a prize for answering a riddle

Best of all, our readers tell us, "Your newsletter is the only one I actually read." So claim your gift today, and please stay in touch!

Sincerely,

Charlotte Ashlock
Steward of the BK Website

Questions? Comments? Contact me at bkcommunity@bkpub.com.

MIX
Paper from
responsible sources
FSC www.fsc.org **FSC® C002589**

Certified

Ⓑ

Corporation
bcorporation.net